ON A COUNTRY ROAD

20 Bicycle Rides in Beautiful and Historic Southeastern Pennsylvania

Barry and Lois Johnston

ON A COUNTRY ROAD

Copyright © 1998 by Barry and Lois Johnston

All rights reserved. No part of this book may be reproduced in any form or by any electronic or mechanical means including information storage and retrieval systems without permission in writing from the publisher, except by a reviewer, who may quote brief passages.

Bicycling is not a risk-free activity. Factors such as weather, road conditions, traffic and other hazards are in a constant state of change. Bicyclists choosing to attempt the tours described in this guidebook should follow safety standards and the state vehicle code, and use good judgment. The authors and publisher of this book can assume no liability for the risks inherent in this sport.

Published by: Greenways Press
              421 Centre Avenue
              Jeffersonville, PA 19403-3222

ISBN: 1-57502-712-7

Printed in the USA by

MORRIS PUBLISHING

3212 East Highway 30 • Kearney, NE 68847 • 1-800-650-7888

Dedicated to our parents, Marian and Kenneth Johnston, and Dorothy and John DeHart, for the encouragement that led us down our first country roads many years ago.

Ride Locations

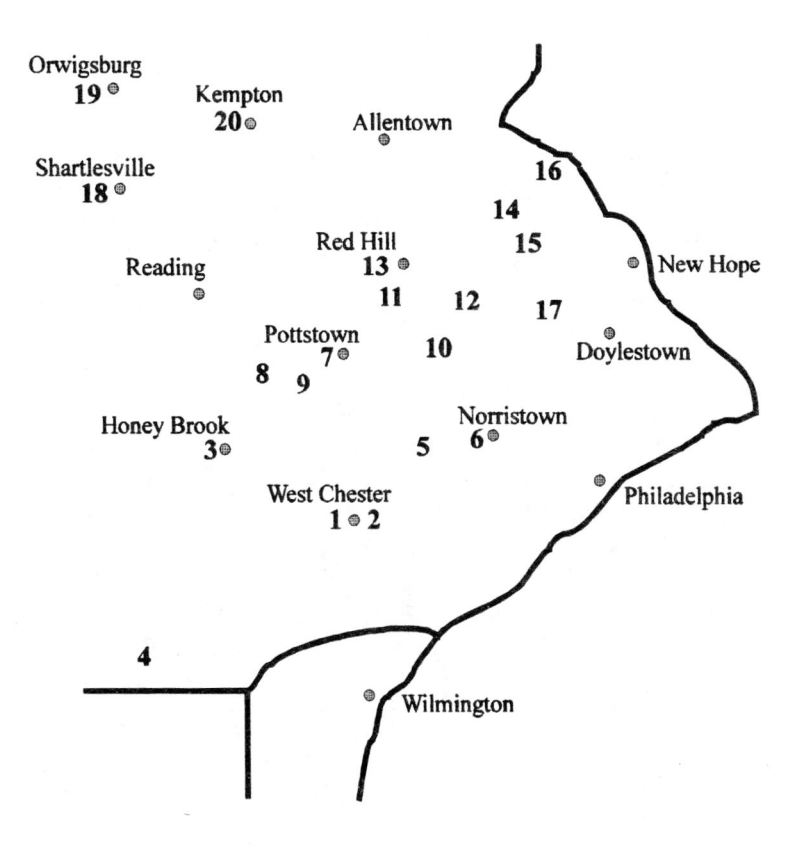

Orwigsburg
19

Kempton
20

Allentown

Shartlesville
18

16

14

Red Hill
13   **15**

Reading   **11** **12**   New Hope

Pottstown   **10**   **17**
7   Doylestown
8 **9**

Honey Brook   Norristown
3   **5**   **6**
                                    Philadelphia
West Chester
1 2

4

Wilmington

Contents

Introduction 7

The Brandywine and Octoraro Valleys
  1. Brandywine Country: A Tour of Central Chester County 11
  2. Artists' Paradise: The Farmlands of Chester County 17
  3. A Honey of a Ride: Honeybrook and Lancaster County 25
  4. Potato Chips and Farmlands: Nottingham Park and
     Lancaster County 29

The Lower Schuylkill Valley
  5. Where Old Meets New: Valley Forge and Chesterbrook 35
  6. Central Montgomery Sampler 41
  7. Furnaces and Forges: Pottstown, Pine Forge and
     Colebrookdale 49
  8. Woodcutters, Iron Masters and Moulders:
     Hopewell Furnace and French Creek 53
  9. A Portrait of Two Villages: St. Peter's and Hopewell 59

The Upper Perkiomen and Delaware Valleys
  10. The "Mountains" of Montgomery County:
      Pennypacker Mills and Spring Mount 63
  11. Deep Creek and the Upper Perkiomen Valley 69
  12. A Little Gem of a Ride: Unami Creek 73
  13. The Chocoholic Ride: Red Hill and Trumbauersville 77
  14. The Less Visited Bucks County 83
  15. Nockamixon's East Shore 89
  16. Rocks and Woods: Ringing Rocks Park, Erwinna
      and Revere 93
  17. The Peace Valley Ride 99

The Upper Schuylkill Valley
  18. America in Miniature: Roadside America and
      Shartlesville 105
  19. Rails and Sails: Leaser Lake and Kempton 109
  20. Following the Tire Tracks of LeMond: Orwigsburg and
      Hawk Mountain 115

Introduction

Much of southeastern Pennsylvania has become a series of rapidly developing suburban communities, complete with tract housing, shopping malls and business parks. However, with a little planning and a little luck, the pastoral scenery that once was typical of the region can still be found. Evansburg and French Creek State Parks challenge the hiker, while Valley Forge and Hopewell Village delight the history buff. Collectors of antiques flock to Skippack and Shartlesville, and bird watchers pursue their hobby at Peace Valley Park and Hawk Mountain.

While this book gives a few hints on pursuing these interests, the main focus is on enjoying southeastern Pennsylvania's back roads by bicycle. Twenty routes have been identified, each highlighting a uniquely beautiful or historical part of the region. While intensive efforts to write this book began in 1996, learning about the roads took much longer. For example, the ride featuring the Orwigsburg and Hawk Mountain areas retraces routes used by one of the authors as he cycled to visit friends prior to getting a driver's license in the early 1970s. The ride leaving Lake Towhee in upper Bucks County is a variation of an after-work fitness ride used by one of the authors. The rides leaving West Chester are modifications of routes used by a charity bike tour the authors coordinated for a number of years.

Except for an extremely challenging road up Hawk Mountain, optional on the Kempton ride, the routes were planned to avoid arduous climbs. However, southeastern Pennsylvania is surprisingly hilly and we found it impossible to design a completely flat ride. On the contrary, we labeled many of the routes "hilly." It just seemed as if the most scenic routes in southeastern

Pennsylvania are in the highlands of the region. Riding a multiple speed bicycle greatly improves the enjoyment of these routes.

Efforts were also made to obtain a reasonable geographical balance. One of the goals of the book was to offer rides within a two hour driving time of Philadelphia's City Hall. However we found some rides outside this radius that were just too pretty to eliminate. For example, the rides leaving Nottingham and Honeybrook provide excellent opportunities to view Pennsylvania's famous Amish country without traveling to the more tourist-oriented central Lancaster County area. Likewise, we just had to include a route in the Shartlesville area, where one can replenish lost calories at a genuine "all you can eat" Pennsylvania Dutch restaurant. Nonetheless, it is conceivable to take an early morning drive to any of the routes, enjoy a day of cycling and be back in Chestnut Hill or Bryn Mawr in time for dinner.

The last thing we want this book to be is a political statement. However, when one cycles in one of these few remaining rural areas, one can't help wondering how to preserve what is left before southeastern Pennsylvania becomes one big commercial zone. Nature trusts and open space purchases have certainly helped to preserve the countryside. Still, more needs to be done, including helping the local farm families preserve a way of life they know and love instead of selling their precious land to developers. We need to start now if we want to keep the back roads of southeastern Pennsylvania enjoyable for bicycling and other outdoor pursuits.

Each ride described in this book is accompanied by a detailed cue sheet and a simple map outlining the route. Points of interest and food stops are noted. Following each ride is a list of telephone numbers for the restaurants and attractions mentioned, as well as information on the nearest bicycle shops. It should be noted, however, that due to the rural nature of some ride locations, the nearest bicycle shop may actually be a number of miles away.

Tips For Safe Bicycling

Bicycling is not a risk-free sport and injuries can occur even to experienced cyclists. There are many factors involved, including the cyclist's skill, road conditions, cars, dogs, the weather, etc. We recommend that the following safety tips be followed, no matter what the skill level of the cyclist may be.

1. Wear a helmet. Approved helmets can lessen or prevent head injuries in the event of a fall.
2. Be sure your bicycle is in good repair.
3. Carry water to avoid dehydration.
4. Obey all the rules of the road.
5. Ride in single file, on the right side of the road.
6. Cross railroad tracks at a right angle.
7. Do not ride after dark unless your bicycle is equipped with appropriate lights.
8. Slow down and use extra caution if the road is wet, sandy, has loose gravel on it, or has potholes.
9. Signal turns in advance and be cautious when making left turns.
10. Stay in control of your bicycle.

Notable Bicycle Events In Southeastern Pennsylvania

Southeastern Pennsylvania plays host to a variety of events each year, attracting cyclists from all over the tri-state area. While we cannot list all of them, here are a few that seem to have withstood the test of time.

Taxing Metric Century
Hosted by the Brandywine Bicycle Club, the routes feature the hilly countryside of northern Chester County. The ride is usually held – when else? – the weekend closest to the April 15 income tax day. Keeping with the theme, the routes are generally marked with dollar signs. Contact the club at PO Box 3162, West Chester, PA 19381.

Montgomery County Mexican Metric Century
Usually held in early May, the ride commemorates the Mexican Independence Day. Hosted by Suburban Cyclists Unlimited, Mexican food is offered at the rest stops. Contact the club at PO Box 401, Horsham, PA 19044.

Freedom Valley Bike Ride
An early June ride, this event is sponsored by the Bicycle Coalition of the Delaware Valley. The coalition is one of the premier advocacy organizations in the region. Contact BCDV on the Web at http://www.libertynet.org/~bcdv/.

Roll & Stroll
This is a ride benefiting the Indian Creek Foundation, a human service agency providing supports for people with mental retardation in western Montgomery and Bucks counties. Usually held in mid to late June, the ride meanders through Upper Perkiomen and Indian Creek Valleys. Contact Indian Creek Foundation at PO Box 225, Harleysville, PA 19438.

USPRO Cycling Championships-Liberty Classic
Early June affords the opportunity of the year to watch the top professional racers strut their stuff in Philadelphia. For early risers, a local charity usually sponsors a ride for non-racers a few hours before the event. It is a great opportunity to ride the famous course and savor the rich variety of neighborhoods that make up the great city of Philadelphia.

Lake Nockamixon Century
Beginning in Horsham, this ride provides a unique opportunity to view the transformation from suburban to rural countryside as one rides from central into upper Bucks County. It is usually held in late September. Contact Suburban Cyclists Unlimited at PO Box 401, Horsham, PA 19044.

Brandywine Country: A Tour Of Central Chester County

- 23.6 miles
- Start and end at Everhart Park within the borough of West Chester
- Terrain: rolling

Highlights

- Roads along the famous Brandywine Creek
- Beautiful horse farms
- Embreeville Mill

The townships just south of West Chester are quintessential Chester County. The landscape is dominated by the meandering Brandywine Creek, with just enough horse farms to paint the countryside picture perfect. While new housing is denser than it was ten years ago, organizations such as the Brandywine Valley Association are doing their part to preserve this historical section of rural Pennsylvania.

West Chester itself is worth exploring if there is time after the ride. The borough is home to a fine state university with beautiful stone buildings at the older end of the campus. West Chester is also the county seat, and the downtown area contains many quaint shops and restaurants. Because of its many fine examples of Greek revival architecture, West Chester was once known as "the Athens of Pennsylvania."

Several food stops have been noted on the cue sheet. We personally recommend Sestrich's Country Store in the center of Unionville. This New England style store can be found at 10.8 miles into the ride. In addition to groceries, Mr. and Mrs. Sestrich have a very nice deli in the back. The sandwiches cannot be beat! Many of the Unionville area's wealthy horse people like to stop in for a midday sandwich, as do the veterinary students from the nearby Bolton Center of the University of Pennsylvania. Please be careful walking inside the store with cleated bicycle shoes. Mr. Sestrich has figured out that there is a correlation between his cyclist patrons and those little black marks he keeps having to scrub off his floor! Unfortunately, Sestrich's Country Store is not open on Sundays.

Getting to Everhart Park

West Chester itself is very accessible from the greater Philadelphia area. Route 202 and Route 3 are the main roads between Philadelphia and West Chester. Once inside the borough, take Gay Street down to North New Street. Make a left turn onto North New Street, cross Market Street and make a right turn onto Miner Street. Everhart Park is a few blocks down on the left. The intersection of Brandywine and Miner Streets forms the northwest corner of the park.

The Ride

0.0	L	From the corner of South Brandywine (on the side of the park) and Miner Streets, make a left turn onto Miner Street.
0.2	S	Leaving the borough of West Chester, cross Bradford Avenue. Miner Street becomes Route 842 west.
1.7	BL	Bear left, staying on Route 842.

3.1	R	Make a right turn, staying on Route 842. Immediately cross the Brandywine Creek.
4.0	L	Make a left turn, staying on Route 842. Again cross the Brandywine Creek.
4.1	L	Make a left turn onto Wawaset Road.
4.2	S	Caution. Cross railroad tracks at right angle. Begin to climb a hill, reaching the crest at 4.7 miles.
6.0	L	Make a left turn, staying on Wawaset Road.
6.5	R	Make a right turn onto Lenape Unionville Road. Do not miss this turn, as a straight will put you on busy Route 152! The county-administered Pocopson Home is on your left.
8.3	BL	Bear left, staying on Lenape Unionville Road.
9.5	R	Make a right turn onto East Doe Run Road.
9.75	BL	Bear left, staying on East Doe Run Road.
10.1	R	Make a right turn onto Unionville Road (Route 82). Caution: busy road! Enter village of Unionville. Sestrich's Country Store will be on the right just before you turn onto Embreeville Road.
10.8	R	Make a right turn onto Embreeville Road.
12.8	BR	Bear right, staying on Embreeville Road.
13.6	S	Pass a KOA Campground on the left.
15.0	R	Make a right turn onto Brandywine Drive. Embreeville Center is on the left, just before making the turn.
17.3	BL	Bear left at the stop sign. Immediately pass Castle Rock Farm.
18.1	R	Make a right turn onto Camp Linden Road.
18.8	R	Make a right turn onto North Wawaset Road.
19.6	L	Make a left turn onto Route 842.
20.1	BR	Bear right, staying on Route 842.

20.5	L	Make a left turn, staying on Route 842.
23.4	S	Straight at stop sign.
23.6	END	End at Miner and South Brandywine Streets.

FYI

Sestrich's Country Store, Unionville (610-347-2225)

Bicycle Shops

Bike Line, West Goshen Shopping Center, West Chester, PA (610-436-8984)

Bike Line, 404 West Lincoln Highway, Exton, PA (610-594-9380)

Exton Bicycles, 315 East Lincoln Highway, Exton, PA (610-363-2727)

West Chester Bicycle Center, 1342 West Chester Pike, West Chester, PA (610-431-1856)

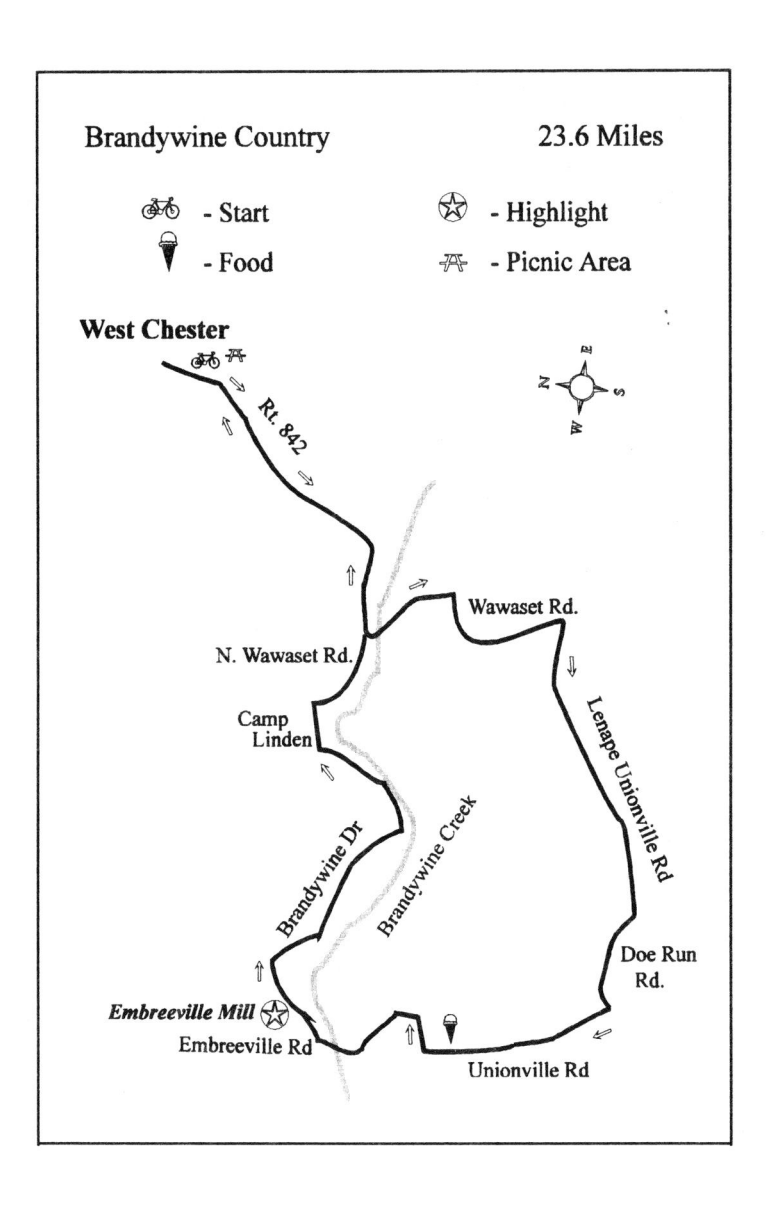

Brandywine Country — 23.6 Miles

Artists' Paradise:
The Farmlands of Chester County

- 48.7 miles
- Start and end at Everhart Park, within the borough of West Chester
- Terrain: rolling with a few steep uphills

Highlights

- Beautiful horse farms.
- Roads along the famous Brandywine Creek.
- Embreeville Mill.
- Covered bridge
- Historic Primitive Hall
- Brandywine Valley Association

Do you want to see the finest horse farms east of Kentucky? The central and western townships of Chester County contain the prettiest horse farms that we have ever seen. No wonder that artists such as the Wyeths have made their homes in this unique part of Pennsylvania. Meandering through the area is Brandywine Creek. The waterway is too small and shallow for anything larger than a canoe or kayak, but it is big enough to be a major attraction for those seeking pastoral beauty.

The ride itself is a longer version of "Brandywine Country." As stated in the opening remarks to that ride, it is recommended that riders spend some time exploring West Chester itself. The borough contains a fine University, with interesting architecture inside the older section of the campus. The shopping district is home to many fine restaurants and interesting shops, as well as the stately county courthouse.

As on the shorter ride, Sestrich's Country Store is the recommended lunch stop. Please read the appropriate section in "Brandywine Country" to find out more about this unique eatery.

Getting to Everhart Park

West Chester itself is very accessible from the greater Philadelphia area. Route 202 and Route 3 are the main roads between Philadelphia and West Chester. Once inside the borough, take Gay Street down to North New Street. Make a left turn onto North New Street, cross Market Street and make a right turn onto Miner Street. Everhart Park is a few blocks down on the left. The intersection of Brandywine and Miner Streets forms the northwest corner of the park.

The Ride

0.0	L	From the corner of South Brandywine (on the side of the park) and Miner Streets, make a left turn onto Miner Street.
0.2	S	Leaving the borough of West Chester, cross Bradford Ave. Miner Street becomes Route 842 west.
1.7	BL	Bear left, staying on Route 842.
3.1	R	Make a right turn, staying on Route 842. Immediately cross the Brandywine Creek.
4.0	S	Go straight. Route 842 will turn left. You are now on North Wawaset Road.
4.8	L	Turn left onto Camp Linden Road.

5.5	L	Make a left turn at T onto Northbrook Road (unmarked). When the turn is made, there will be horse pastures on either side of the road and a farm ahead.
6.3	R	Make a right turn onto Brandywine Drive. This is a very scenic, but narrow road. Watch for traffic.
8.65	L	Make a left turn onto Route 162 (unmarked). After making the turn Embreeville Center will be on the left side of the road. At one time, this was an institution for people with mental retardation. However, the center officially closed in 1997, and the buildings and grounds now have multiple uses. For instance, many of the fields are now used for soccer leagues.
9.4	S	Straight at stop sign, staying on Route 162 (also known as Embreeville Road).
10.0	S	Pass a KOA Campground on right. Use caution at the railroad tracks.
10.3	S	Pass the Embreeville Mill, a favorite subject of local artists.
10.75	R	Make a right onto Powell Road.
10.8	R	Make a right turn onto Brandywine Creek Road.
11.9	R	Make a right turn onto an unmarked (and un-named) road. Immediately cross a very scenic concrete bridge.
12.0	L	Make a left turn onto Youngs Road (the sign pointing the opposite direction will say "Harvey's Bridge Road.")
12.1	L	Make a left turn onto Laurel Road.
14.2	S	Cross Strasburg Road. Laurel Road becomes Mortonville Road. Find food and drink at Marty's Pub on right.

15.0	L	Make a left turn, staying on Mortonville Road. (The road sign says "Mortonville Road," but local maps show this as Creek Road).
16.4	L	Inside the little borough of Modena, make a left turn onto Union Street. Use caution. A stone wall on the left makes it a little hard to see up the road.
16.5	L	Make a left turn onto South Brandywine Avenue.
16.55	R	Make a right turn onto Hephzibah Road. Ascend the steepest hill of the ride.
17.35	R	Make a right turn onto Strasburg Road.
17.4	L	Make a left turn onto Frog Hollow Road (local maps show this as "Hephzibah Hill Road.") Houdeeney's Pizza is on the corner. After enjoying a pizza, enjoy a downhill almost two miles long!
19.2		Cross a covered bridge. Caution! The floor of this bridge is VERY uneven. When we were affiliated with a charity ride that used this road, we used to make cyclists walk through the bridge because of the uneven flooring.
19.2	L	After going through the bridge, make a left turn onto Covered Bridge Road.
19.6	R	Make a right turn onto Dupont Road.
19.8	L	Make a left turn onto Doe Run Road (Route 82). Caution: busy road.
20.3	R	Make a right turn onto Route 841 south (Chatham Road).
20.5	R	Make a right turn onto Chapel Road.
21.3	S	Go straight at the stop sign.
22.5	BL	Bear left onto Gum Tree Road. Do NOT make the sharp left turn onto Rosenvick Road. Enter the tiny village of Gum Tree.

23.2	R	Make a right turn onto Friendship Church Road.
25.3	L	Make a left turn onto Friends Meetinghouse Road (unmarked). CAUTION. This road is easy to miss because it is unmarked. A little further up Friendship Church Road is a stop sign and an intersection with a busy road. This is Route 10. If you are here, go back. You went too far.
26.8	S	Go straight at the stop sign.
27.1	L	Make a left turn at the Y, staying on Friends Meetinghouse Road.
27.9	BR	Bear right.
28.7	L	Make a left turn onto Green Lawn Road.
30.4	R	Make a right turn onto North Chatham Road.
31.2	S	Go straight, staying on Route 841 South. Pass historical Primitive Hall on left. Primitive Hall is a large Georgian country house built in 1738.
31.9	BR	Bear right.
32.0	L	Make a left turn onto Route 926 (Street Road).
32.8	R	Make a right turn onto Howellmoore Road.
33.75	L	Make a left turn onto London Grove Road.
35.1	L	Make a left turn onto Spencer Road. Pass the Stroud Water Research Center on left.
36.2	L	Left onto Newark Road.
36.5	S	Go straight at the stop sign.
37.6	R	Make a right turn onto Upland Road (Route 842).
39.65	R	Make a right turn, staying on Route 842. Enter the village of Unionville.
39.9		Sestrich's Country Store is on the left. Use caution if you decide to cross the road to visit the store.

40.0	L	Make a left turn, staying on Route 842 (Wawaset Road).
42.9		Pass Northbrook Orchards on the left. Refreshments can be purchased anytime, but it is really worthwhile stopping in during the harvest season. Try a cider donut!
43.2		Pass the Brandywine Valley Association. Often there are special events going on here on weekends. It is worth the stop.
44.5		Caution. Cross the railroad track at a right angle.
44.6	BL	Bear left, crossing the bridge over the creek.
44.7	R	Make a right turn, staying on Route 842.
45.2	BR	Bear right.
45.6	L	Make a left turn, staying on Route 842.
48.5	S	Go straight at the stop sign.
48.7	END	End ride at the corner of Miner and South Brandywine Streets.

FYI

Brandywine Valley Association, West Chester (610-793-1090)
Northbrook Orchards, West Chester (610-793-1210)
Sestrich's Country Store, Unionville (610-347-2225)

Bicycle Shops

Bike Line, West Goshen Shopping Center, West Chester, PA (610-436-8984)

Bike Line, 404 West Lincoln Highway, Exton, PA (610-594-9380)

Exton Bicycles, 315 East Lincoln Highway, Exton, PA (610-363-2727)

West Chester Bicycle Center, 1342 West Chester Pike, West Chester, PA (610-431-1856)

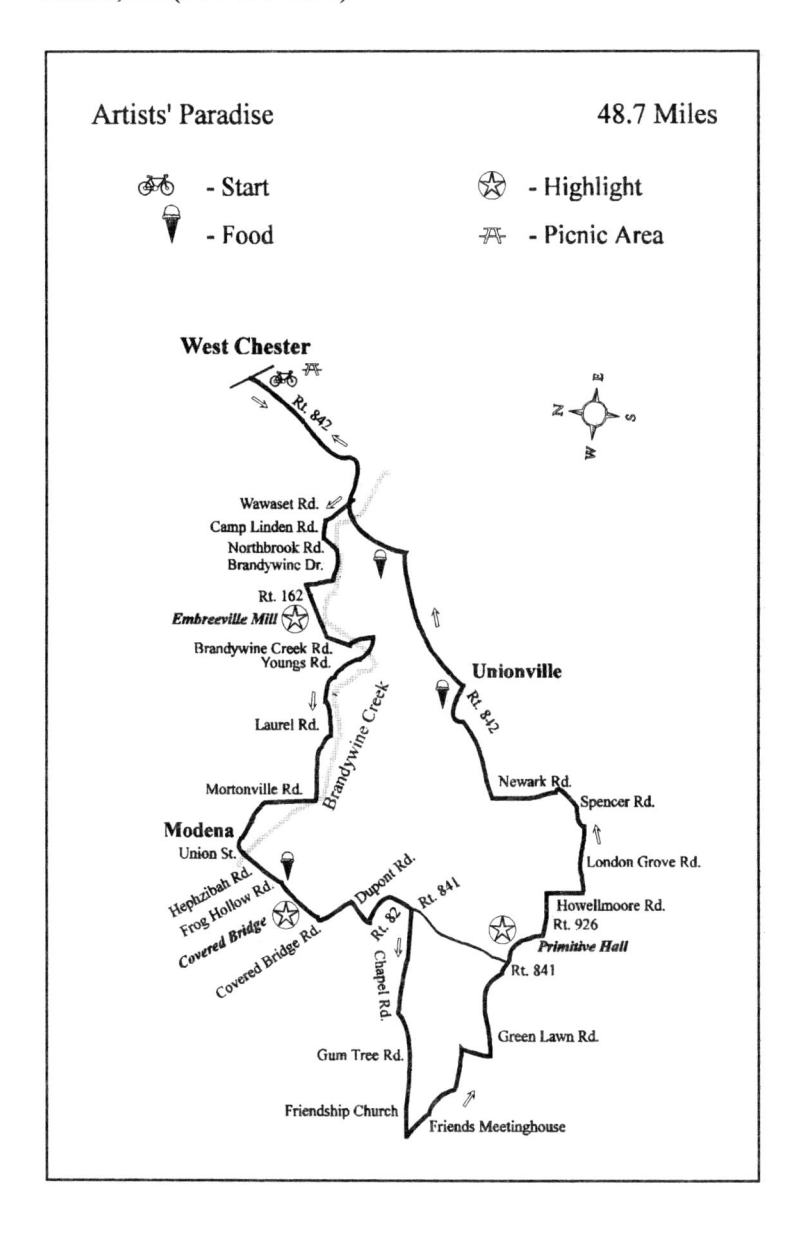

A Honey Of A Ride: Honeybrook And Lancaster County

- 18.8 miles
- Start and end in parking lot on Firehouse Lane, Honeybrook, across the street from the library and municipal building
- Terrain: very hilly

Highlights

- Horse drawn carriages
- Beautiful Amish farm country

Just like the Nottingham Park ride, this route starts in Chester County and takes a quick dip into Lancaster County. The ride goes just far enough into Lancaster County to see all the scenery associated with this beautiful part of Pennsylvania. But, at the same time, the route stays well to the east of the area frequented by tour buses and heavy traffic.

Within the village of Honeybrook, there are a variety of places from which food can be purchased. Sometimes it is also possible to find an impromptu food stand set up by an Amish family along the road.

Getting to Honeybrook

Honeybrook can be reached by getting off the turnpike at Morgantown and taking Route 23 west to Route 10 south. An alternative from Philadelphia's western suburbs is to take Route 30 west to Route 322 West. The parking lot on Firehouse Lane can be seen from Route 10, a block south of the intersection of Routes 10 and 322. Traveling south on Route 10, there are signs for the municipal building and the library on the right. The parking lot is on the left.

The Ride

0.0	R	Riding out of the parking lot onto Firehouse Lane, turn right (corner of Firehouse Lane and Railroad Street).
0.15	R	Make a right turn onto Maple Street.
0.25	L	Make a left turn onto Park Street.
0.4	S	Go straight at the stop sign.
3.0	R	Turn right onto Beaver Dam Road.
4.95	S	Go straight at the stop sign.
6.8	BR	Bear right onto Byerly Road
7.55	L	Make a left turn onto Churchtown Road.
7.8	R	Make a right turn onto Plank Road.
8.6	R	Make a right turn onto Blank Road (no, this is not a typo. There actually is a Plank Road and a Blank Road).
10.3	L	Make a left turn onto Wanner Road.
10.9	L	Make a left turn onto Cambridge Road.
11.3	S	Go straight on Seldonridge Road (Cambridge Road bears left).
11.4	S	Go straight at the stop sign.
12.0	S	Go straight. Seldonridge becomes Meetinghouse Road.
12.6	R	Make a right turn onto Meadeville Road.

13.6	L	Make a left turn onto Gault Road.
13.65	R	Make a right turn onto Meadeville Road.
14.2	L	Make a left turn onto Red Hill Road.
14.3	R	Make a right turn onto Meadeville Road.
17.4	R	Make a right turn onto West Walnut Road.
18.2	S	Cross Route 10. Caution. This is a busy intersection.
18.35	L	Make a left turn onto Maple Street.
18.7	L	Make a left turn onto Firehouse Lane
18.85	END	End ride by making a left turn into the parking lot.

Bicycle Shops

Bike Line, Airport Village Shopping Center, Coatesville, PA (610-380-4553)

Bike Line, 117 Rohrerstown Road, Lancaster, PA (717-394-8998)

Downington Bicycle Shop, 833 West Lancaster Avenue, Downingtown, PA (610-269-5626)

Honey of a Ride

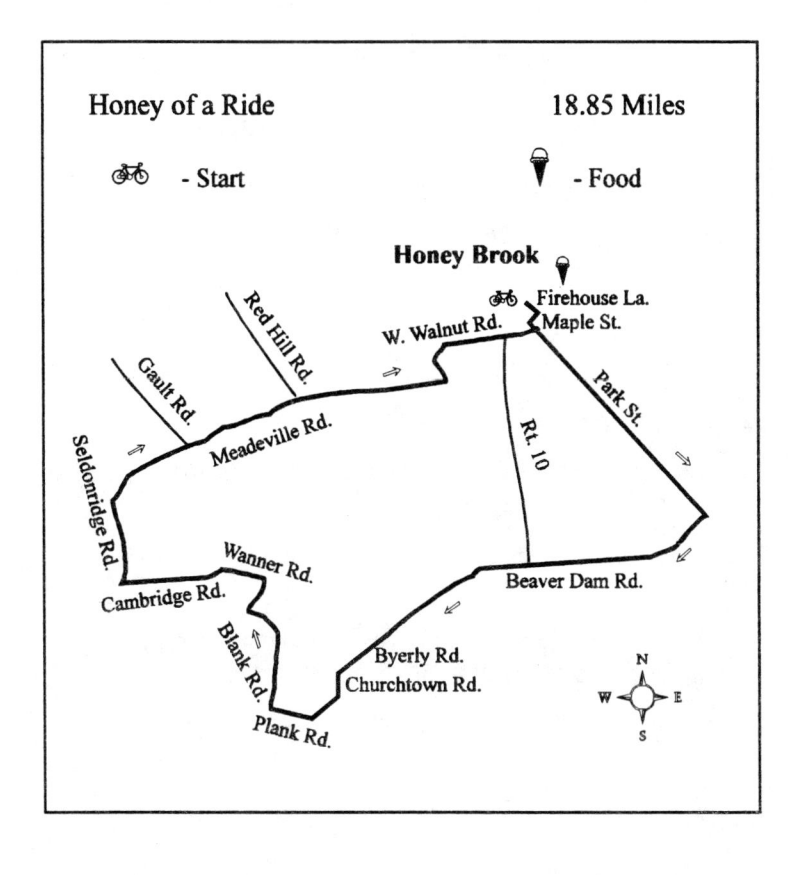

18.85 Miles

🚲 - Start   🍦 - Food

Honey Brook

- Firehouse La.
- Maple St.
- Red Hill Rd.
- W. Walnut Rd.
- Gault Rd.
- Park St.
- Meadeville Rd.
- Rt. 10
- Seldonridge Rd.
- Wanner Rd.
- Cambridge Rd.
- Beaver Dam Rd.
- Blank Rd.
- Byerly Rd.
- Churchtown Rd.
- Plank Rd.

Potato Chips And Farmlands: Nottingham Park And Lancaster County

- 28.6 miles
- Start and end at Nottingham County Park
- Terrain: hilly

Highlights

- Nottingham County Park
- Horse-drawn carriages
- Beautiful Amish farm country
- Covered bridge
- One room schoolhouse

Lancaster County has developed a much deserved reputation for bicycling. Its many rural roads wander through lush pastures, occasionally dotted with covered bridges and one room Amish schoolhouses. However, within the more popular areas, cyclists often need to share the road with tour buses and other seasonal traffic. This ride, as well as the ride leaving Honeybrook, attempts to explore the eastern tip of Lancaster County, which is an area that the tourists often miss.

Like the Honeybrook ride, the tour starts and ends in Chester County. Nottingham Township is famous as the home of Herr Foods, a popular provider of potato chips and other snack foods (free tours are available at the factory by appointment). The township's other prized possession is a lovely county park. Its picnic pavilions are often used as food stops for local century rides coming through the park.

For people wishing to extend their stay, a Bed and Breakfast called "Little Britain Manor" is at the six mile mark of the ride. Innkeepers Fred and Evelyn Crider invite their guests to awaken to the aroma of coffee, eggs, bacon, homemade biscuits and sweet bologna. The inn boasts four bedrooms, each decorated in a distinctive country flavor.

For day touring, lunch and snack items can be purchased within the tiny town of Little Britain, located at the intersection of Brown Road and Route 272 at 6.3 miles on the tour.

Getting to Nottingham County Park

Nottingham County Park, operated by the county of Chester, is most easily reached from the Philadelphia area by taking Route 1 to the Nottingham Exit, just south of Oxford, PA. After exiting Route 1, follow the brown and white signs for Nottingham County Park. The main gate is on Park Road on the left. The ride begins at the main gate.

The Ride

0.0	L	From the main gate, make a left turn onto Park Road.
1.5	S	Continue straight after stop sign. Park road becomes Lee's Bridge Road. Watch for traffic coming from right.
1.9	R	Make a right turn onto Freemont Road.
3.3	BL	Cross the Lancaster County Line. Bear left after crossing bridge.
4.3	S	Continue straight on Freemont Road, which becomes Brown Road. Pass the Little Britain Manor on left at 6.0 miles.

6.3	S	Straight, crossing Route 272. Brown Road becomes Little Britain (North) Road.
7.4	R	Make a right turn onto Jackson Road.
8.1	BR	Bear right onto Spring Hill Road.
8.4	R	Make a right turn at the T (unmarked).
8.8	L	Make a left turn onto Shady 337 Road.
9.4	L	Make a left turn onto King Pen Road.
10.0	S	Stay on King Pen Road, following sign saying, "covered bridge ahead."
10.2	R	Make a right turn, going through the covered bridge.
10.4	BL	Bear left onto White Rock Road.
11.4	R	Make a right turn onto Hill Road. Pass Amish one room schoolhouse on left.
11.7	S	Straight, staying on Hill Road.
11.9	R	Make a right turn onto Street Road. Caution: traffic on left is coming over the crest of a hill.
12.8	L	Make a left turn onto Kirkwood Pike (Route 472).
13.0	R	Make the first right turn onto Morrison Mill Road. The sign is partially obscured.
13.4	R	Make a right turn onto Sproul Road.
14.6	R	Make a right turn onto Rosedale Road.
15.4	L	Make a left turn onto Street Road.
16.0	S	Cross the Chester County Line.
16.6	R	Make a right turn onto Newcomer's Road.
17.1	R	Make a right turn at the T onto Homeville Road (unmarked).
18.25	R	Make a right turn onto Cream Road (unmarked). On the right are the Cream Gift Shop and Robert

		Trent Hogge, Cabinetmaker. The gift shop is worth visiting.
19.1	L	Make a left turn onto Scroggy Road (unmarked).
19.95	R	Make a right turn onto Jackson School Road.
20.2	BL	Bear left, staying on Jackson School Road. Enjoy a long downhill!
21.25	L	Make a left turn onto Lancaster Pike (unmarked). Caution: busy road. A reservoir will be on the right.
21.4	R	Make a sharp right onto Mt. Vernon Road.
22.5	BL	Bear left at the stop sign. Mt. Vernon Road becomes Bethel Road.
22.9	R	Make a right turn onto Street Road.
23.6	L	Make a left turn at the T onto Forge Road (unmarked).
25.05	R	Make a right turn onto Hopewell Road (unmarked). This is the first right turn past Calvary Road.
26.25	L	Make a left turn onto Glen Roy Road. Immediately cross Route 272.
27.1	S	Straight, staying on Glen Roy Road.
28.0	R	Make a right turn onto Cemetery Road.
28.35	L	Make a left turn onto Park Road.
28.6	END	End ride at main gate of Nottingham County Park.

FYI

Herr Foods, Nottingham (800-284-7488)
Little Britain Manor, Little Britain (717-529-2862)
Nottingham County Park, Nottingham (610-932-9195)

Bicycle Shops

Bike Line, 212 East Main Street, Newark, DE (302-368-8779)

Bike Line, 117 Rohrerstown Road, Lancaster, PA (717-394-8998)

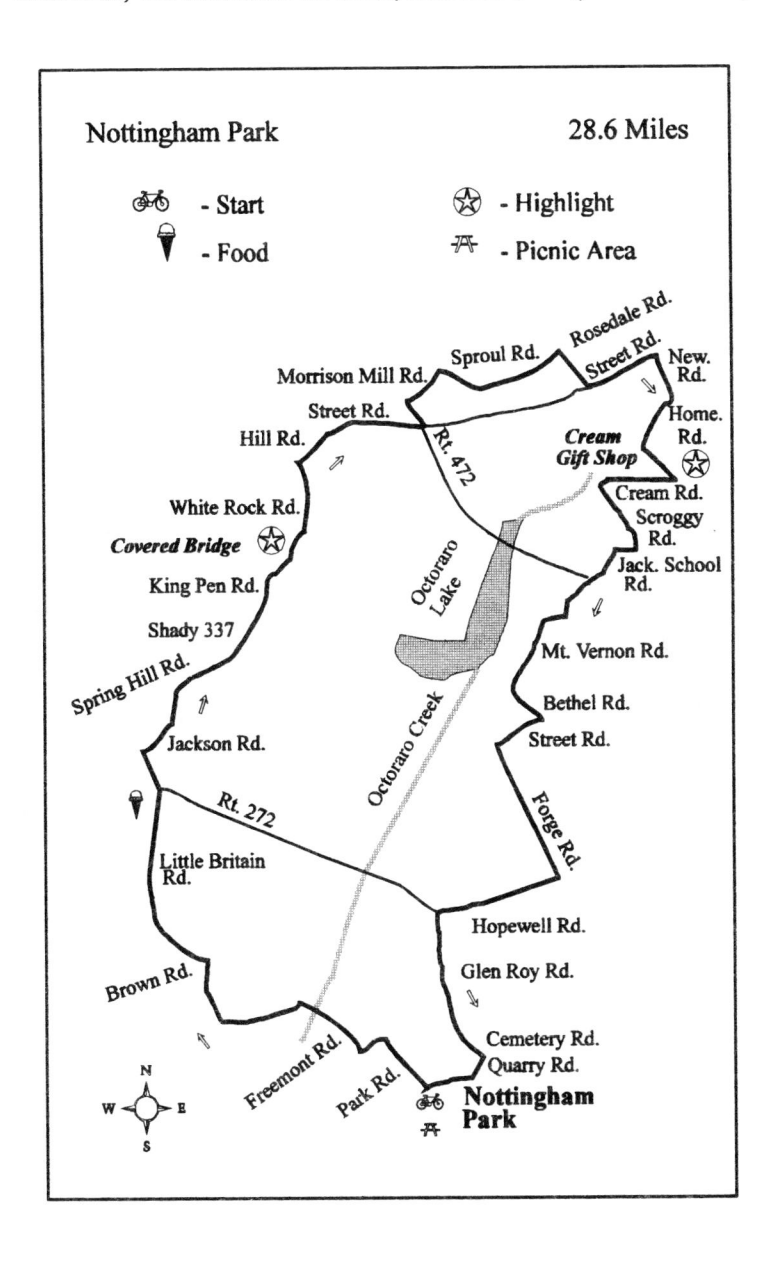

Where Old Meets New: Valley Forge and Chesterbrook

- 15.3 miles, with up to 44 additional miles possible on bikeway
- Start and end at the Betzwood Picnic Area of Valley Forge National Historical Park
- Terrain: rolling, but optional trip on bikeway is flat

Highlights

- Valley Forge National Historical Park
- Great Valley Mill
- Knox Covered Bridge
- Diamond Rock Octagonal School
- Philadelphia to Valley Forge Bikeway

Valley Forge is well known for its place in American history. It was here that George Washington and his army survived, barely, the bitter winter of 1777-78. Today, the extensive remains and reconstructions bring the dramatic story to life for the many visitors to the National Historical Park. The park is also a beautiful place of hills and meadows, with hiking trails, picnic areas, and a six mile bike path around the perimeter. A stop at the Visitor Center is recommended, and, if time permits, a tour of the park by car or bicycle.

The ride passes by Diamond Rock School at the 6.6 mile point. This structure is one of five octagonal schools built in the region during the early 1800's. It is constructed of stone, and measures ten feet to each of the eight sides. At the 7.5 mile point, the ride passes Great Valley Mill. A mill has stood at this spot since 1710, and the current structure was erected in 1859. It was in active service as late as 1950.

From the historic Valley Forge area, the ride continues into Chesterbrook, a modern planned community of four thousand homes. With a shopping center and a number of high-tech industries, Chesterbrook is a model of a self-contained community.

Food is available on the ride at stores and restaurants in the Chesterbrook Village Center, at the ten mile point in the ride. Tables and grills are located in the Betzwood Picnic Area, at the start/finish point.

The length of the ride may be extended by turning right instead of left on the bikeway at the end of the ride. The Philadelphia to Valley Forge Bikeway follows the Schuylkill River through Norristown, Conshohocken, and Spring Mill to Manayunk. It detours onto Manayunk streets for a short way, and then continues along Kelly Drive all the way to the Philadelphia Art Museum. Riders may travel as far as they wish before turning around and retracing their route back to the Betzwood Picnic Area. The distance to Philadelphia from Valley Forge on the bikeway is 22 miles.

Getting to Valley Forge

From Philadelphia, take either the Pennsylvania Turnpike or the Schuylkill Expressway to King of Prussia, and get on Route 422 west. Continue on Route 422 to the exit for Route 363 (Trooper Road). Make a left turn onto Trooper Road at the end of the exit ramp, continue across the overpass, and turn right into the Betzwood Picnic Area.

Parking is also available at the lower lot behind the Visitor Center in the park. Reach it from Route 422 by following the signs for Valley Forge Park. Exit the parking lot on the right side by walking around the gate, and make a left onto County Line Road, joining the ride at the .7 mile point.

The Ride

0.0	S	Exit the Betzwood parking lot by following the paved bike path, which begins next to the bulletin board.
0.05	R	Make a right turn on the bike path, following the sign for the river crossing.
0.3	L	Make a left turn after leaving the bridge across the Schuylkill River, following the bikeway signs.
0.5	R	Make a right turn at stop sign onto Route 23. Caution: busy road!
0.5	L	Make an immediate left turn onto County Line Road (unmarked). A sign points to "Maintenance Area".

Optional: To visit the Visitor Center, turn left at this point onto the bike path rather than continuing on County Line Road. Travel on the bike path about .5 mile to the Visitor Center on the right. If you would like to see a bit more of the park, continue past the Visitor Center on the bike path until you reach the National Memorial Arch. Just past the Arch, turn left onto Outer Line Drive, rejoining the ride at the 2.0 mile point. Caution: the bike path in the park is popular with walkers and joggers, and tends to be crowded on weekends.

1.9	L	Make a left turn at the T onto North Gulph Road (unmarked).
2.0	R	Make a right turn onto Outer Line Drive, just before the National Memorial Arch. Outer Line Drive parallels the bike path.
3.6	R	Make a right turn at the stop sign onto Route 252.
4.0	L	Make a left turn, going through Knox Covered Bridge and onto Yellow Springs Road.

6.6	S	Pass Diamond Rock School on the right.
6.7	BL	Bear left onto North Valley Road.
7.5	S	Pass Great Valley Mill on the left.
7.7	L	Make a left turn onto Swedesford Road.
8.5	L	Make a left turn at the traffic light onto Duportail Road.
9.5	L	Make a left turn at the traffic light onto Chesterbrook Boulevard.
11.2	S	Continue straight at the traffic light onto Sullivan Road.
11.5	L	Make a left turn at the T onto Anthony Wayne Drive.
11.6	R	Make a right turn at the stop sign onto Walker Road (unmarked).
12.1	L	Make a left turn at the stop sign onto Thomas Road.
13.0	L	Make a left turn at the T onto North Gulph Road. Reenter Valley Forge National Historical Park. Use caution on the bricks by the National Memorial Arch.
13.5	R	Make a right turn onto County Line Road (unmarked).
14.8	R	Make a right turn onto Route 23.
14.8	L	Make an immediate left turn onto an unmarked road. Follow the river crossing signs.
15.0	R	Make a right turn onto the bikeway to cross the river.
15.25	L	Make a left turn onto the bikeway and follow it to the parking area.

Optional: To extend the ride, turn right rather than left onto the bikeway. The bikeway can be followed for as long as desired, and continues for 22 miles to Philadelphia.

15.3 END End at Betzwood Picnic Area.

FYI

Valley Forge National Historical Park, Valley Forge (610-783-1077)

Bicycle Shops

Bean's Bikes Inc., 10 West Lancaster Avenue, Paoli, PA (610-640-9910)

Bikefit Inc., 1987 West Main Street, Jeffersonville, PA (610-539-8393)

Bike Line, Paoli Shopping Center, Paoli, PA (610-647-8023)

Bike Line, 740 West DeKalb Pike, King of Prussia, PA (610-337-3003)

Bike Line, 711 Nutt Road, Phoenixville, PA (610-935-9111)

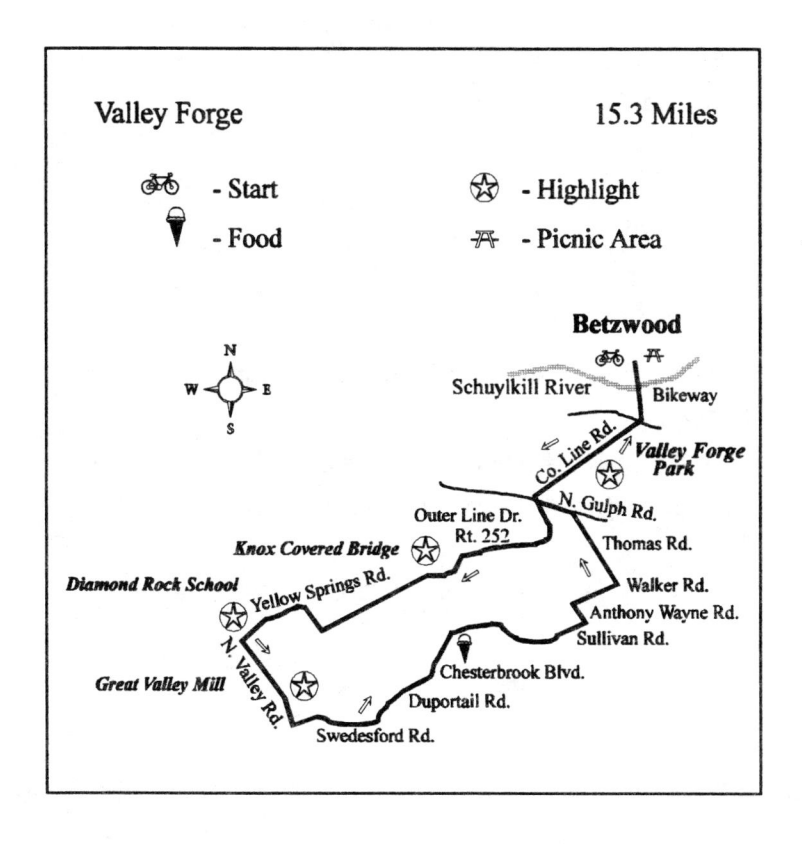

Valley Forge   15.3 Miles

🚲 - Start   ⭐ - Highlight
🍦 - Food   🛱 - Picnic Area

Central Montgomery Sampler

- 30.5 miles (32.25 miles with optional side trip to Skippack)
- Start and end at the Norristown Farm Park
- Terrain: rolling hills with a few steep climbs

Highlights

- Norristown Farm Park
- Evansburg State Park
- Olympic champion's horse farm
- Village of Skippack

Central Montgomery County is an area of contrast and paradox. Much of its rural character has been lost to suburban development. However, narrow corridors of beautiful woods and fields still exist. At the eastern end of the ride, one can spot the tops of Philadelphia's highest skyscrapers from Upper Farm Road. In clear contrast, the western end of the ride is rural enough in character to boast a state park.

The ride begins at the Norristown Farm Park, the newest addition to the Montgomery County Park System. The farm once belonged to Norristown State Hospital, and raised food for the psychiatric patients at the facility. The patients also worked on the farm as a form of therapy.

At the 12.4 mile point of the ride is Vintage Farm, the home of Michael Matz. Matz, a long time member of the United States Equestrian Team, won a silver medal in the 1996 Olympics. In addition to his equestrian achievements, Matz is credited with saving the lives of two children during a plane crash in Souix City, Iowa,

The optional trip into the village of Skippack is worth taking for the interesting array of shops and restaurants. The village has a very fine reputation for antique stores as well as arts and crafts shops. While the village also contains many outstanding restaurants, most are a little too formal to visit in cycling attire. A delightful exception is Mal's American Diner, visible from the intersection of Route 73 and Store Road. Famous for its breakfast entrees, Mal's also has a fantastic lunch menu. The restaurant is a favorite destination for local bike clubs, and the owner plans to install a bicycle rack. Right next to Mal's is Skippack Bike and Blade, a small but friendly bicycle shop.

Another food stop option is Merrymead Farm, located just off the 23.8 mile mark. The excitement here centers on ice cream and other dairy treats. However, one can also find baked goods and fresh farm produce (in season). Live farm animals complete the ambiance of this lively dairy bar.

Getting to Norristown Farm Park

Norristown Farm Park is located on Germantown Pike, between Swede Street and Whitehall Road, just northwest of the borough of Norristown. Traveling west on Germantown Pike, the entrance is on the left, just opposite North Wales Road. There is a sign, but unfortunately it is well past the intersection. The best way to find the entrance is to look for the sign indicating North Wales Road. There is also a sign for Barley Sheaf Townhouses, which one passes before coming to the Farm Park.

The Ride

0.0	R	From the parking lot of the Montgomery County Farm Park Visitor's Center (facing the Visitor's Center), make a right turn onto Upper Farm Road.
0.9	BL	Bear left, staying on Upper Farm Road.
1.1	S	Walk your bicycle around the gate. The gate marks the grounds of Norristown State Hospital.
1.15	BL	Bear left, staying on Upper Farm Road.
1.2	R	Make a right turn onto Beech Drive.
1.4	R	Make a right turn onto Sterigere Street (leaving the State Hospital).
1.6	L	Turn left onto Colonial Avenue.
2.1	R	Turn right onto Marshall Street.
2.8	R	Turn right onto Kramer Drive.
2.9	L	Turn left onto Palmer Drive.
3.0	R	Turn right onto Burnside Avenue.
3.1	L	Turn left onto Chestnut Avenue.
3.7	R	Turn right onto Stable Road.
4.0	L	Turn left onto Oakland Avenue.
4.1	R	Turn right onto Trooper Road.
4.9	S	Straight, crossing Germantown Pike. Begin a steep ascent.
5.8	L	Turn left onto Woodland Avenue.
6.2	S	Straight, crossing Valley Forge Road. Caution: busy road.
6.4	L	Turn left onto Dell Road.
6.8	L	Turn left onto Quarry Hall Road.
7.0	R	Turn right onto Mill Road. Enjoy a pleasant descent!

8.5	R	Turn right onto Grange Avenue.
9.0	L	Turn left onto Water Street.
10.0	R	Turn right and walk your bicycle around the barricade, using the pedestrian bridge to cross Skippack Creek. Continue walking on the path on the other side of the creek.
10.1	S	Rejoin Mill Road straight ahead. The entrance to Evansburg State Park is just to the right. This road leads to picnic areas and a youth hostel.
10.8	L	Turn left onto Evansburg Road.
11.6	R	Turn right onto Township Line Road. You will soon pass Vintage Farm on the right.
12.6	R	Turn right onto Hildebeitel Road.
13.2	R	Turn right onto Mill Road.
13.5	L	Turn left onto Collegeville Road.
14.0	R	Turn right onto Landis Road. View airport just before turning.
14.1	L	Turn left onto Collegeville Road.
15.9	R	Turn right onto Hallman Avenue.
16.3	L	Turn left onto Evansburg Road.
16.7	S	At the traffic light go straight, crossing Route 73.
17.1	L	Turn left onto Township Line Road.
17.5	R	Turn right onto Store Road.
		Optional side trip to village of Skippack: To get to Skippack, make a left turn onto Store Road. Take Store Road .87 miles into the village. To rejoin the ride, simply turn around and go back to the intersection of Store and Township Line Roads. Go straight on Store Road.
19.7	R	Turn right onto Rittenhouse Road. View golf course on right.
20.1	R	Turn right onto Old Forty Foot Road.

20.5	L	Turn left onto Old Morris Road.
21.4	R	Turn right onto Bustard Road.
21.7	L	Turn left onto Kriebel Road.
22.6	R	Turn right onto Trumbauer Road. Immediately cross a pretty stone bridge.
22.9	L	Turn left onto Morris Road.
23.8	S	Go straight at the traffic light, crossing Valley Forge Road. Make a right turn here to go to Merrymead Farm. Valley Forge Road is very busy and extreme caution needs to be taken in making the left turn into Merrymead. To rejoin the route, retrace Valley Forge Road to the intersection of Valley Forge and Morris Roads, making a right turn onto Morris Road.
25.1	R	Turn right onto Berks Road.
26.4	S	Go straight, crossing route 73. Caution: busy road!
27.2	L	Turn left onto Bean Road. Use caution crossing railroad tracks just before North Wales Road.
28.3	R	Turn right onto North Wales Road.
29.1	S	Go straight crossing Township Line Road. A Wawa store is on the left.
30.0	S	Go straight, crossing Germantown Pike to enter the Norristown Farm Park.
30.3	R	Make a right turn onto Upper Farm Road.
30.5	END	End the ride at the Visitors Center of Norristown Farm Park.

FYI

Evansburg State Park, Collegeville (610-489-3729)
Mal's American Diner, Skippack (610-584-0900)
Merrymead Farm, Lansdale (610-584-4410)
Norristown Farm Park, Norristown (610-270-0215)

Bicycle Shops

Bike and Blade, 4002 Skippack Pike, Skippack, PA (610-222-0560)

Bikefit Inc., 1987 West Main Street, Jeffersonville, PA (610-539-8393)

Bikesport, 325 West Main Street, Trappe, PA (610-489-7300)

Pedaller Bike Shop, 840 West Main Street, Lansdale, PA (610-361-2909)

Steve's Bike and Fitness, 1510 DeKalb Pike, Blue Bell, PA (610-275-4010)

Central Montgomery Sampler — 30.5 Miles

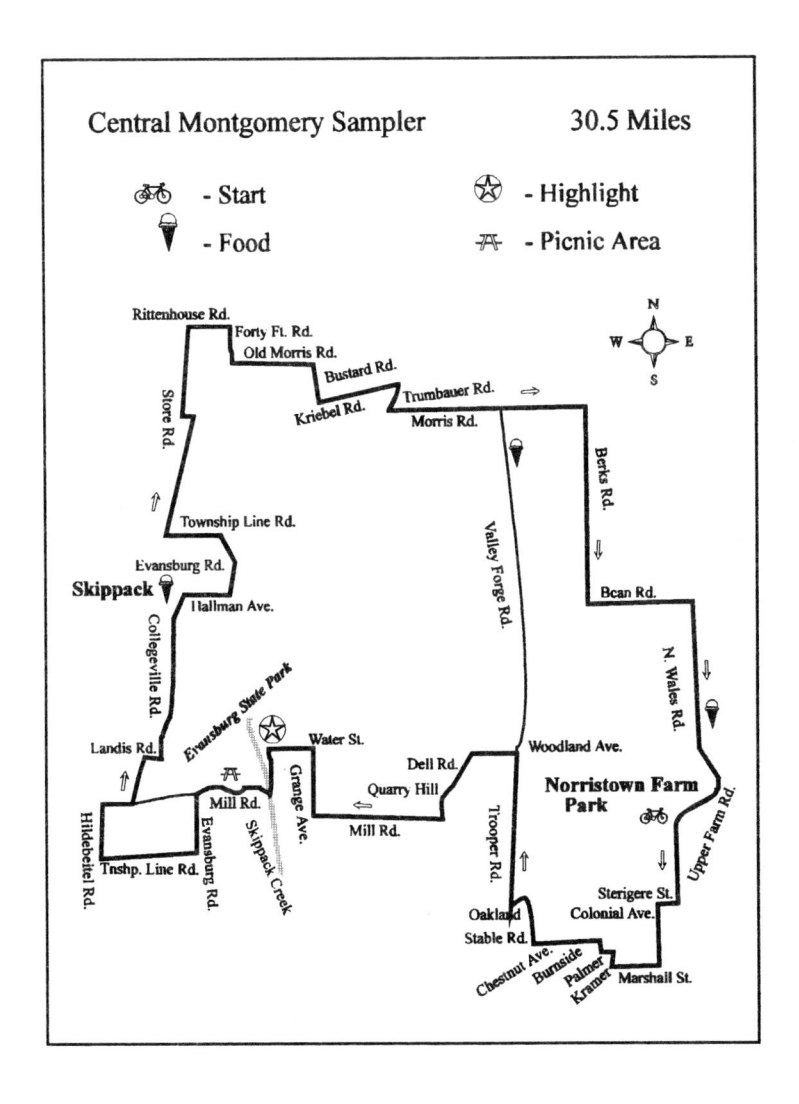

- 🚲 - Start
- 🍦 - Food
- ⭐ - Highlight
- ⛨ - Picnic Area

Skippack

Rittenhouse Rd., Forty Ft. Rd., Old Morris Rd., Bustard Rd., Kriebel Rd., Trumbauer Rd., Morris Rd., Store Rd., Township Line Rd., Evansburg Rd., Hallman Ave., Collegeville Rd., Berks Rd., Bean Rd., Valley Forge Rd., N. Wales Rd., Landis Rd., Evansburg State Park, Water St., Dell Rd., Woodland Ave., Upper Farm Rd., Mill Rd., Grange Ave., Quarry Hill, Mill Rd., Skippack Creek, Hildebeitel Rd., Tnshp. Line Rd., Evansburg Rd., Trooper Rd., Norristown Farm Park, Sterigere St., Oakland, Colonial Ave., Stable Rd., Chestnut Ave., Burnside, Palmer, Kramer, Marshall St.

Furnaces And Forges: Pottstown, Pine Forge And Colebrookdale

- 14.4 miles
- Start and end at Pottstown's Memorial Park
- Terrain: rolling with one steep climb

Highlights

- Memorial Park
- Beautiful Manatawny Creek
- Pine Forge Academy

The tri-county area just northwest of Pottstown played a significant role in the early iron industry of a very young nation. John Potts, for whom the town is named, was a very wealthy Ironmaster. His mansion, situated at the corner of King Street and Route 100, is very close to the start of this ride and worth seeing if time permits.

After leaving Memorial Park, the ride travels up the Manatawny Valley to Pine Forge. Subsequent to its conversion to a school in 1945, Pine Forge was one of many historical iron forges in the area. The forge also functioned as a stop on the Underground Railroad. The nationally renowned Pine Forge Academy Choir practices in a building that was originally the stable for the old forge.

Before winding back to Pottstown, the ride visits the picturesque village of Colebrookdale, once the home of Colebrookdale

Furnace. Built in 1720, Colebrookdale Furnace is probably the first blast furnace to operate in Pennsylvania. The furnace was named after the Colebrook Furnace in England.

Two restaurants, Cynthia's Greshville Inn and the Little Oley Tavern, are noted along the route. Also there is a lovely little creek-side picnic area on Manatawny Street between Pottstown and Pine Forge. The Ice House Deli, located on Manatawny Street near the beginning of the ride, is a good source of food.

Getting to Pottstown's Memorial Park

From the Philadelphia area, take Route 422 west to Pottstown. Exit Route 422 at Hanover Street, taking Hanover Street into the center of town. Turn left onto King Street. Follow King Street to Manatawny Street, making a left turn onto Manatawny. Memorial Park is on the left of Manatawny Street, with a parking lot close to the Vietnam Veterans Memorial area. Additional parking can be found on side streets, as well as at the Gruber Swimming Pool, just off the King Street entrance to the park.

The Ride

0.0	L	From the Memorial Park parking lot on Manatawny Street, make a left turn onto Manatawny Street.
2.0	S	Cross the Berks County line.
2.4	S	Caution: Cross railroad tracks at right angle to the tracks.
3.2	L	Make a left turn at the T onto Pine Forge Road (unmarked). Signs will point to Pine Forge and Greshville. Pine Forge Academy is about half a mile up the road.
4.1	R	Make a right turn onto Douglas Drive.
7.5	R	Make a right turn onto Route 562.

7.9	R	Make a right turn onto Greshville Road (sign on the left). This is the first right turn after turning onto Route 562. Cynthia's Greshville Inn is on the left on Route 562.
8.7	S	Caution: railroad tracks at the bottom of the hill.
8.75	BL	Bear left, staying on Greshville Road.
9.0	R	Make a right turn onto Farmington Avenue, entering the little town of Colebrookdale.
9.2	BR	Bear right onto Colebrookdale Road. The Little Oley Tavern is on the right. Ascend a very short, steep hill followed by a long, not quite uninterrupted descent. Caution: stop sign at bottom of the hill, just before Manatawny Street.
12.0	L	Make a left turn onto Manatawny Street.
14.4	END	End ride at the parking lot for Memorial Park on Manatawny Street.

FYI

Cynthia's Greshville Inn, Boyertown (610-367-6994)
Ice House Deli, Pottstown (610-326-9999)
Little Oley Tavern, Boyertown (610-367-2353)

Bicycle Shop

Bike Line, Pottstown Plaza, Pottstown, PA (610-970-1866)

52

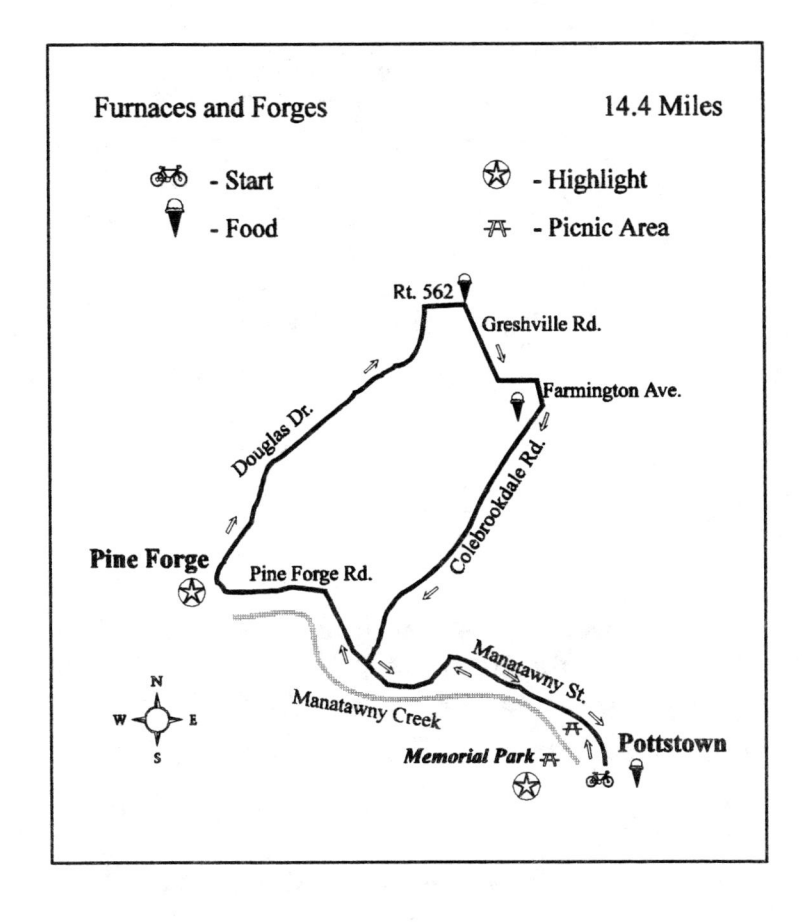

Woodcutters, Ironmasters and Moulders: Hopewell Furnace And French Creek

- 14.0 miles (14.8 miles with optional side trip to Hopewell Lake)
- Start and end at Hopewell Furnace National Historic Site
- Terrain: hilly

Highlights

- Hopewell Furnace National Historic Site
- French Creek Sheep and Wool Company
- French Creek State Park
- Interesting collection of railroad equipment

During the late 18th century, southeastern Berks County was home to many of the finest charcoal-fueled iron furnaces in the nation. However, by the mid 19th century, newer methods of producing iron were discovered and most of the furnaces disappeared. In 1938, the National Park Service restored the old Hopewell Furnace and began administering the area as a National Historic Site. Today, the restored furnace, waterwheel, blast machinery, ironmaster's mansion and other miscellaneous structures remind visitors of a thriving industry that once flourished in this unique part of Pennsylvania.

Almost surrounding Hopewell Furnace is French Creek State Park. When Hopewell was in operation, the area now occupied by the park produced the charcoal necessary to fuel the large blast furnace. While woodcutters chopped the trees, colliers burned the wood in hearths to produce the needed charcoal. Today, the park supports a diverse ecosystem, while providing outdoor recreation opportunities to the ever expanding population of southeastern Pennsylvania. Activities that can be enjoyed in the Park include hiking, camping, swimming, fishing, boating, orienteering and disc golf (sometimes known as "Frisbee golf").

A grocery store is noted at the 8 mile mark of the ride. Scott's Run and Hopewell Lakes contain picnic areas very suitable for eating a carry-along lunch.

For individuals wishing to do a longer ride, it should be noted that this ride can easily be combined with the St. Peters and Hopewell Village ride. After completing the loop, pick up the St. Peters ride by making a right turn from Route 345 onto Hopewell Road instead of turning left into the driveway for Hopewell Village. This is the 7.4 mile mark of the St. Peters ride.

Getting to Hopewell Furnace National Historic Site

From the Philadelphia area, take the Pennsylvania Turnpike to the Route 100-Downingtown Interchange. After leaving the turnpike, take Route 100 north to Route 23. Make a left turn onto Route 23 west. Make a right turn onto Route 345 north. Hopewell Furnace is on the left, about a mile and a half past the south entrance of French Creek State Park.

The Ride

0.0	S	Begin in the parking lot of Hopewell Furnace National Historic Center, just opposite the visitors' center. Ride out the driveway (called Mark Bird Lane). For a small fee, one can pick apples in season in the orchard surrounding the parking lot.
0.3	R	Make a right turn onto Route 345 south.

0.8	S	Cross the Chester County line.
1.6	S	Pass the French Creek Sheep and Wool Company on the left. A sheepskin bicycle seat cover is among the products the company makes and sells.
1.7	R	Make a right turn and enter French Creek State Park on South Entrance Road (brown sign says "French Creek State Park").
2.9	L	Make a left turn onto Park Road

Optional Side Trip to Hopewell Lake: To get to Hopewell Lake, make a right turn onto Park Road. Follow Park Road .4 mile to the Lake. To rejoin ride, simply turn around and ride back to the intersection of South Entrance Road and Park Road. Continue straight on Park Road at this intersection.

5.4	R	Make a right turn onto Kline Road.
6.0	R	Make a right turn onto Red Hill Road.
6.4	L	Make a left turn at the T onto Cold Run Road (unmarked).
7.8	R	Make a right turn onto Route 82, into the tiny village of Geigertown.
8.0	R	Make a right turn onto Geigertown Road. After making the turn, Shirey's Groceries is on the right. An interesting collection of old railroad equipment can be seen on the left.
8.7	R	Make a right turn onto Kratz Road.
9.6	L	Make a left turn onto Fire Tower Road.
9.95	S	Reenter French Creek State Park.
10.1	BL	Bear left. A right turn will take you up to the fire tower. It would be worth the climb if the tower were open, but unfortunately, it is closed to the

		public. There is still a picnic area there, with grills and a fireplace.
10.8	BR	Bear right at sign pointing towards Main Park Area, Scott's Run Lake, and Campground. Scott's Run Lake itself is on a marked one-way side road on the right and is worth visiting.
11.8	L	Make a left turn at the T onto Park Road (unmarked, but there is a sign pointing to Route 345.)
12.9	R	Make a right turn onto Route 345.
13.5	R	Make a right turn onto Mark Bird Drive, entering Hopewell Furnace National Historic Site.
14.0	END	End ride in parking lot opposite visitors' center.

FYI

French Creek Sheep and Wool Co., Elverson (610-286-5700)
French Creek State Park, Elverson (610-582-9680)
Hopewell Furnace National Historical Site, Elverson (610-582-8773)
Shirey's Groceries, Birdsboro (610-286-9835)

Bicycle Shops

Bike Line, 3925 Perkiomen Avenue, Exeter, PA (610-779-7120)
Bike Line, Pottstown Plaza, Pottstown, PA (610-970-1866)

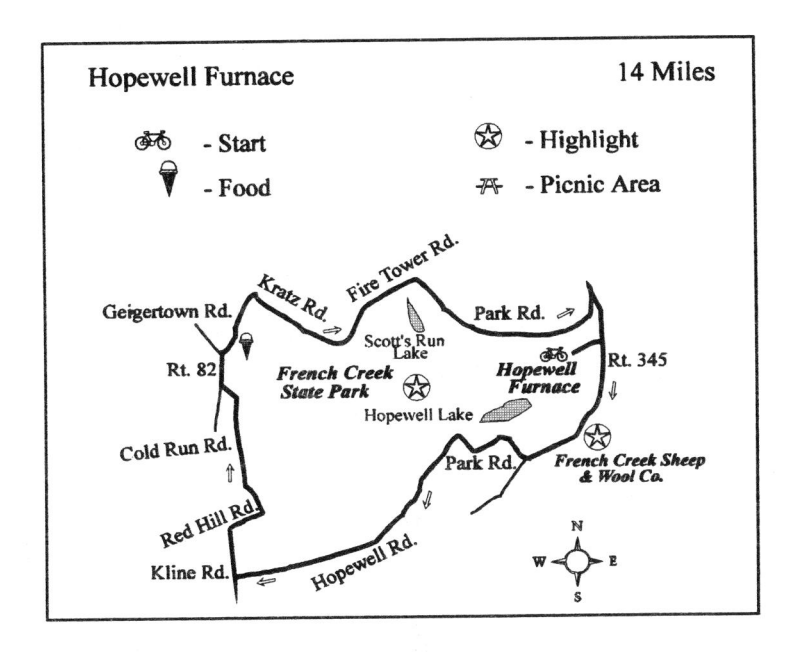

Hopewell Furnace
14 Miles

- 🚴 - Start
- 🍦 - Food
- ⭐ - Highlight
- 🎪 - Picnic Area

Kratz Rd., *Fire Tower Rd.*, *Park Rd.*, *Geigertown Rd.*, *Rt. 82*, *Cold Run Rd.*, *Red Hill Rd.*, *Kline Rd.*, *Hopewell Rd.*, *Park Rd.*, *Rt. 345*

Scott's Run Lake, *French Creek State Park*, *Hopewell Furnace*, Hopewell Lake, *French Creek Sheep & Wool Co.*

A Portrait Of Two Villages: St. Peters And Hopewell

- 10.7 miles (11.3 miles with optional trip to Hopewell Village)
- Start and finish at St. Peters Village
- Terrain: rolling with a few steep climbs

Highlights

- St. Peters Village
- Beautiful horse farms
- French Creek Sheep and Wool Company
- Hopewell Furnace National Historic Site

St. Peters Village is one of the many quaint little arts and crafts centers located in the western ends of the suburban counties. At the south end of the one-street town is a handsome Victorian inn that features fine dining in a lovely setting. Walking north, it is easy to find an interesting variety of stores selling anything from teddy bears to fudge. While researching this ride, we talked with the shopkeeper at the fudge store and found out that bicycle enthusiasts come from as far away as Harrisburg to enjoy this interesting part of the state. Behind the shops is a beautiful glen, highlighted by a fast-running boulder-filled creek.

At the other end of the ride is Hopewell Furnace National Historic Site. Operated by the federal government, the site is a restored early 19th century iron making village and includes a furnace, waterwheel, ironmaster's mansion and other buildings.

For those wishing a longer ride, it should be noted that this route can easily be combined with the Hopewell Furnace and French Creek ride. After visiting the French Creek Sheep and Wool Company, turn around and travel south on Route 345. Only a tenth of a mile on the right is a brown sign that says "French Creek State Park." Turn right into the park here, joining the Hopewell Furnace and French Creek Ride at the 1.7 mile mark.

Food is available at a number of snack bars in St. Peters Village.

Getting to St. Peters Village

From the Philadelphia area, take Route 422 west to Route 100 south (just south of Pottstown). Continue on Route 100 south to Route 23 west. After passing through Coventryville, start looking for a sign pointing to St. Peters Village on the right. Warwick County Park will be on the left. Turn onto St. Peters Road at the sign to get to the village. The parking lot from which the ride starts is at the opposite end of the village.

The Ride

0.0	R	From the south end of the St. Peters Village parking lot (next to Rosie's Café), make a right turn onto St. Peters Road, passing through the village.
0.6	R	Make a right turn onto Route 23. This is a busy road, but it has a nice shoulder.
2.0	R	Make a right turn onto Trythall Road. The sign is impossible to see, but there is a prominent green and white sign for Warwick Woods Campgrounds just before the road.
3.5	L	Make a left turn onto Harmonyville Road.
3.7	BL	Bear left, staying on Harmonyville Road.

4.5	BL	Bear left, staying on Harmonyville Road. Travel through State Game Lands.
5.4	R	Make a right turn onto Pine Swamp Road (Route 345).
6.1	S	Pass the French Creek Sheep and Wool Company on the right. Among the products the company makes and sells is a sheepskin bicycle seat cover.
7.4	R	Make a right turn onto Hopewell Road.
9.3	R	Make a right turn onto Keim Road. Pass pretty horse farm on the left.
9.5	L	Make a left turn onto Harmonyville Road. The sign says "Bradley's Corner."
9.9	R	Make a right turn onto St. Peters Road.
10.7	END	End the ride at the St. Peters Village parking lot

FYI

French Creek Sheep and Wool Co., Elverson (610-286-5700)
French Creek State Park, Elverson (610-582-9680)
Hopewell Furnace National Historical Site, Elverson (610-582-8773)
St. Peters Inn, St. Peters (610-469-3809)

Bicycle Shops

Bike Line, 3925 Perkiomen Avenue, Exeter, PA (610-779-7120)
Bike Line, Pottstown Plaza, Pottstown, PA (610-970-1866)

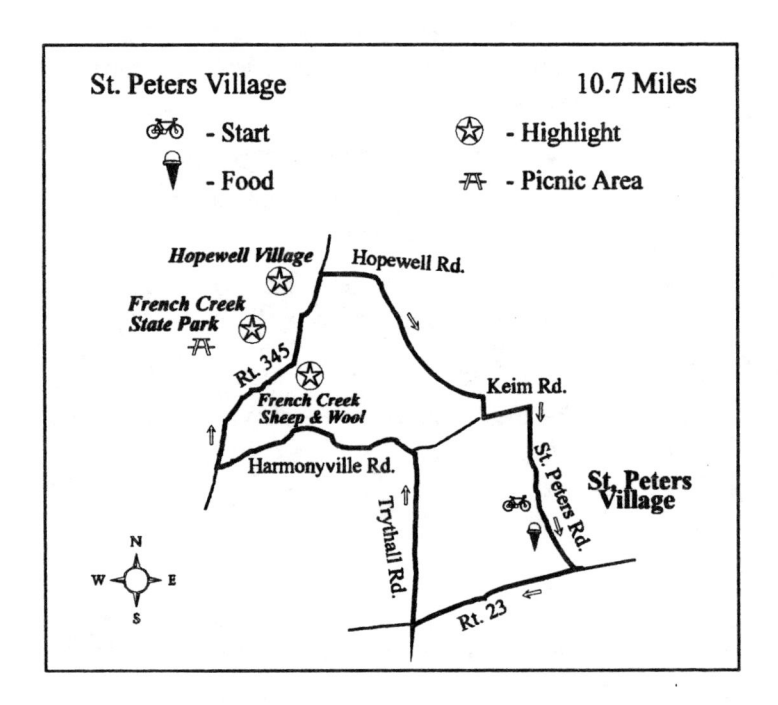

St. Peters Village

10.7 Miles

- 🚴 - Start
- 🍦 - Food
- ✡ - Highlight
- 🪑 - Picnic Area

The "Mountains" Of Montgomery County: Pennypacker Mills And Spring Mount

- 16.3 miles
- Start and end at historic Pennypacker Mills
- Terrain: hilly

Highlights

- Pennypacker Mills Mansion
- Spring Mountain Ski Area
- Bergey's Mill Farmstead

There is no area within southeastern Pennsylvania that is truly mountainous. However, the hills surrounding the Schwenksville-Spring Mount Area contain just enough vertical drop to justify a ski area. Spring Mountain never claims to compete in the same market as Aspen. Yet its close proximity to Philadelphia and its western suburbs has earned the little enterprise a loyal following.

For the cyclist, the climb over Spring Mountain certainly is not Le'Alpe d"Huez. But this climb, as well as others along the route, will make for a vigorous ride.

The ride begins at Pennypacker Mills, a historical site preserved by the Montgomery County Department of History and Cultural Arts. The mansion on the property was home to Samuel W. Pennypacker, a distinguished lawyer, historian, farmer and

Governor of Pennsylvania. From February, 1901 to May, 1902, renovations were made to transform what was then a stone German farmhouse into a colonial mansion. In 1985, four years after its purchase, the county opened the house and grounds to the public. The county sponsors numerous special events on the property throughout the year, including watercolor painting workshops, an Earth Day Celebration, and natural heritage walks.

The ride also passes another historical home, Bergey's Mill Farmstead, at the 12.7 mile mark. Tours are available by appointment.

At 3.3 miles, a lunch stop is noted at Justa Pizza Plus. For cyclists wishing to carry their lunch, there is a lovely picnic area just before crossing the bridge at 10.6 miles on Camp WaWa Road.

Getting to Pennypacker Mills

From Philadelphia's northwestern suburbs, take Route 73 west through Blue Bell, Center Point and Skippack. Just before coming to the bridge over the Perkiomen Creek and the intersection with Route 29, turn right onto Haldeman Road and an immediate left into Pennypacker Mills.

The Ride

0.0	S	Begin the ride at the parking lot of Pennypacker Mills Mansion. Ride out the driveway back towards Haldeman Road. (The driveway is a dirt road, but very well maintained).
0.3	L	Make a sharp left turn onto Haldeman Road. Pass the Perkiomen Valley Watershed Association on the right. View the mansion on the left.
0.7	L	Make a left turn onto Dieber Road.

1.0	L	Make a left turn onto Pennypacker Road. There is a brief, but pretty view of Schwenksville on the left.
1.4	R	Make a right turn at the stop sign onto Schwenksville Road (unmarked).
2.1	BL	Bear left, staying on Schwenksville Road.
2.5	L	Make a left turn onto Spring Mount Road. Look for sign for Spring Mountain Ski Area. Pass the ski area on the left.
3.3	R	Inside the village of Spring Mount, make a right turn onto Main Street. Justa Pizza Plus is on the right.
3.7	S	Continue straight at stop sign.
4.1	R	Make a right turn onto Schwenk Road.
4.8	R	Make a right turn onto Salford Station Road.
6.3	S	Entering the tiny town of Salford, go straight. Salford Station Road becomes Salford Street.
6.4	S	Continue straight on Salford Street (sign says "Quarry Road").
7.5	R	Make a right turn onto Old Skippack Road. Pass through the little town of Salfordville, with pretty views on both sides of the road.
9.6	BR	Bear right. Old Skippack Road becomes Salfordville Road.
10.3	R	Make a right turn onto Camp WaWa Road.
10.6	S	Cross an iron bridge. Caution: the bridge is very slippery if wet. There is a pretty picnic area on the right, just before the bridge.
11.5	L	Make a left turn onto Haldeman Road.
12.2	S	Keep going straight. Haldeman Road becomes Bergey's Mill Road.
12.7	S	Pass the Bergey Mill Farmstead on the left.

13.1	R	Make a right turn onto Cross Road.
14.4	R	Make a right turn onto Route 73. Caution: Route 73 is very busy, but has a wide shoulder.
16.0	R	Make a right turn onto Haldeman Road and an immediate left turn into Pennypacker Mills.
16.3	END	End the ride in the parking lot of the mansion.

FYI

Bergey Mill Farmstead, Schwenksville (610-257-6010)
Justa Pizza Plus, Springmount (610-287-6030)
Pennypacker Mills, Schwenksville (610-287-9349)

Bicycle Shops

Bikesport, 371 Main Street, Harleysville, PA (610-256-6613)

Tailwind Bicycle Shop, 160 Main Street, Schwenksville, PA (610-287-7870)

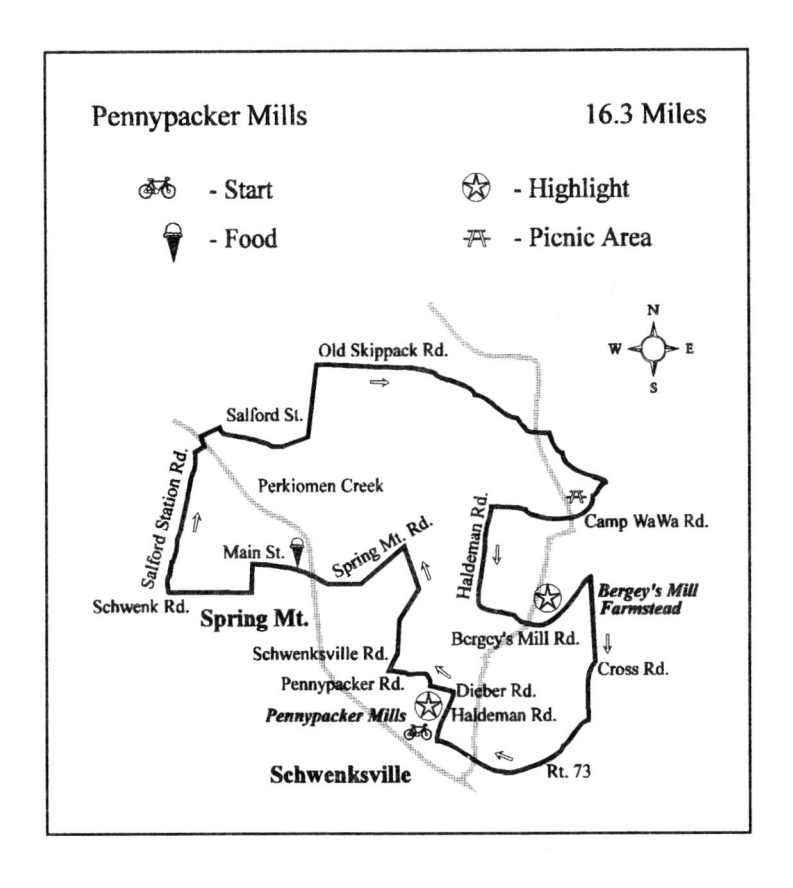

Pennypacker Mills 16.3 Miles

- 🚲 - Start
- 🍦 - Food
- ⭐ - Highlight
- 🪑 - Picnic Area

Old Skippack Rd.
Salford St.
Salford Station Rd.
Perkiomen Creek
Main St.
Spring Mt. Rd.
Haldeman Rd.
Camp WaWa Rd.
Schwenk Rd.
Spring Mt.
Bergey's Mill Farmstead
Bergey's Mill Rd.
Schwenksville Rd.
Cross Rd.
Pennypacker Rd.
Dieber Rd.
Pennypacker Mills
Haldeman Rd.
Schwenksville
Rt. 73

Deep Creek And The Upper Perkiomen Valley

- 10.1 miles
- Start and end at the Upper Perkiomen Valley Park
- Terrain: hilly

Highlights

- Upper Perkiomen Valley Park
- Upper Montgomery County farm country
- Beautiful Deep Creek Lake

One of the largest and most popular parks within the Montgomery County System is the Upper Perkiomen Valley Park. The park was founded in 1939 on 425 acres of land purchased by the county. Eventually additional lands were purchased until the park reached its present size of 563 acres. Activities at the park include canoeing and boating on Deep Creek Lake, hiking, and picnicking. Concerts are sometimes held in the summer, and in winter the park is popular for sledding, cross country skiing, and ice skating.

The ride visits the tiny village of Perkiomenville, famous at the turn of the century for a rather large cattle auction which took place behind the present day Perkiomenville Hotel. According to historians, cattle were brought in by railroad from as far away as Ohio for the auction. The ride also visits the Deep Creek Valley, which played a significant part in the early industrial development of the area. However, today very little evidence exists of industry. Much of the valley is either woodlands or home lots.

Food is not available along the route. However, Upper Perkiomen Valley Park is a wonderful place for a picnic before or after the ride. Picnic tables and grills are available there.

Getting to Upper Perkiomen Valley Park

Traveling north on Route 29, there are signs for Upper Perkiomen Valley Park on the left hand side of the road, just before entering the Borough of Green Lane. Cross the bridge after turning left from Route 29. The parking lot at Snyder and Deep Creek Roads is just a little beyond the guard house. Upper Perkiomen Valley Park is also accessible from Route 63. Going east on Route 63, go through the Borough of Green Lane. While still inside the borough, turn left onto Route 29 and follow the directions above.

The Ride

0.0	R	From the parking lot at the corner of Snyder and Deep Creek Roads, make a right turn onto Deep Creek Road.
0.5	R	Inside the little village of Perkiomenville, make a right turn onto Perkiomenville Road.
2.4	R	Make a right turn onto Little Road (marked by sign on left). Little Road runs along the top of a ridge with nice views of the valley on the left.
3.6	R	Make a right turn onto Township Line Road
3.7	L	Make a left turn onto Little Road (unmarked). It is the first left turn after turning onto Township Line Road.
5.0	BL	Bear left, staying on Little Road.
5.1	R	Make a right turn, staying on Little Road.

5.8	R	Make a right turn onto Schultz Road. If you come to a stop sign, you are at Route 663. Go back to Schultz Road. You went too far!
6.65	S	Go straight. Schultz Road becomes Deep Creek Road.
7.35	S	Go straight at the stop sign, staying on Deep Creek Road.
9.5	S	Go straight at the stop sign, staying on Deep Creek Road.
10.1	END	End the ride at the parking lot on the corner of Snyder and Deep Creek Roads.

FYI

Upper Perkiomen Valley Park, Green Lane (215-234-4528)

Bicycle Shops

Bike Line, Route 202 & 309 & 463, Montgomeryville, PA (215-361-7900)

Bikesport, 371 Main Street, Harleysville, PA (610-256-6613)

Tailwind Bike Shop Ltd., 351 Main Street, Pennsburg, PA (215-541-4949)

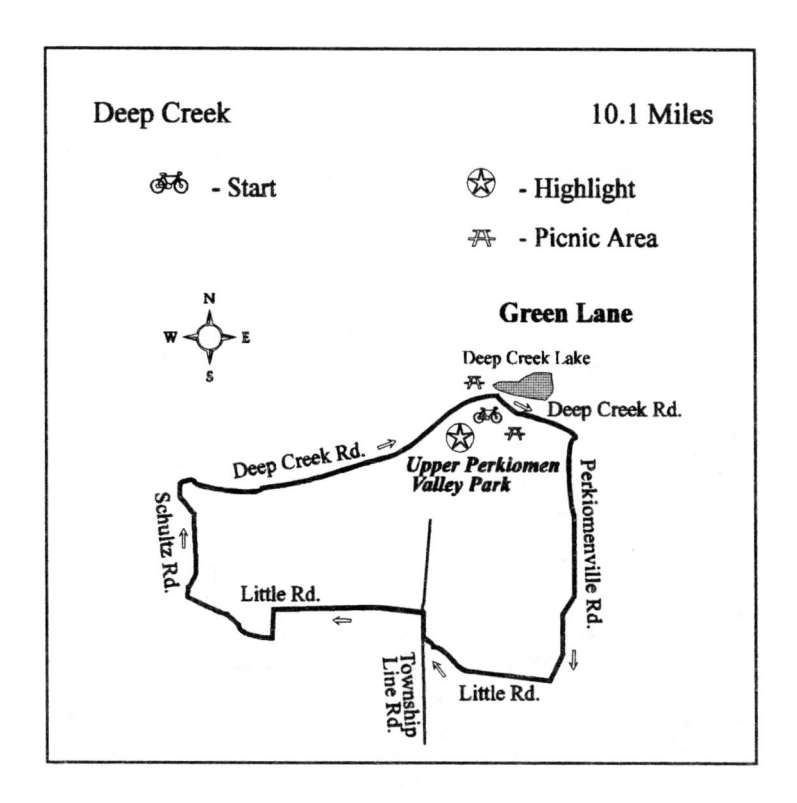

Deep Creek

10.1 Miles

🚲 - Start   ⭐ - Highlight   ⛱ - Picnic Area

Green Lane

Deep Creek Lake
Deep Creek Rd.
Deep Creek Rd.
Upper Perkiomen Valley Park
Schultz Rd.
Perkiomenville Rd.
Little Rd.
Township Line Rd.
Little Rd.

A Little Gem Of A Ride: Unami Creek

- 9.6 miles
- Start and finish at community park in Sumneytown
- Terrain: rolling, with one long, difficult climb at the start

Highlights

- Unami Creek
- Thick forests

Just north of the Upper Perkiomen lies a fast running, boulder strewn stream called Unami Creek. Next to the creek runs Swamp Creek Road. However, the terrain is anything but swampy. The creek speeds down a hillside, occasionally interrupted by small dams. The ride is a little tough as it moves out of the valley, using roads just west of Unami Creek. However, no hard work goes unrewarded. The last four to five miles of the ride cruise gradually downhill through woods and along the beautiful creekside. There are not any places to purchase food along the route. Your best bet is to bring a picnic lunch to enjoy along one of the many scenic spots on the creek! Food is available in Sumneytown.

The road next to the creek may be busy during the first couple weekends of fishing season. Early in the fishing season may not be the best time to do the ride, unless both fishing and cycling are on the agenda! The ride is especially pretty a little later, in May, when dogwood trees and wildflowers bloom along the road.

Getting to the Community Park in Sumneytown

The park in Sumneytown, located on Swamp Creek Road, has no name, but is easy to find nonetheless. From the Kulpsville/Harleysville area, travel west on Route 63 until you get to Sumneytown. Within the village of Sumneytown, make a right turn onto Geryville Pike. Very shortly thereafter, make a right turn onto Swamp Creek Road. The park is practically at the intersection of Swamp Creek Road and Geryville Pike.

The Ride

0.0	L	Standing in the park, facing Swamp Creek Road, make a left turn onto Swamp Creek Road.
0.1	R	Make a right turn onto Geryville Pike. Ascend a mile long hill.
1.0	R	Make a right turn onto Upper Ridge Road. Pass the Delmont-Hart Scout Reservation.
4.2	R	Make a right turn, staying on Upper Ridge Road.
4.9	R	Make a right turn onto Swamp Creek Road. Nice scenery ahead!
6.1	L	Make a left turn, staying on Swamp Creek Road. Cross a stone bridge over Swamp Creek.
6.3	BR	Bear right, staying on Swamp Creek Road.
9.35	L	After crossing another pretty stone bridge, turn left, staying on Swamp Creek Road.
9.6	END	End back at Community Park on the left.

Bicycle Shops

Bikesport, 371 Main Street, Harleysville, PA (610-256-6613)

Hatfield Bike Shop, 1625 Hatfield Valley Road, Hatfield, PA (215-368-8383)

Scooter's Bike Shop, 130 N. Main Street, Souderton, PA (215-723-5909)

Tailwind Bike Shop Ltd., 351 Main Street, Pennsburg, PA (215-541-4949)

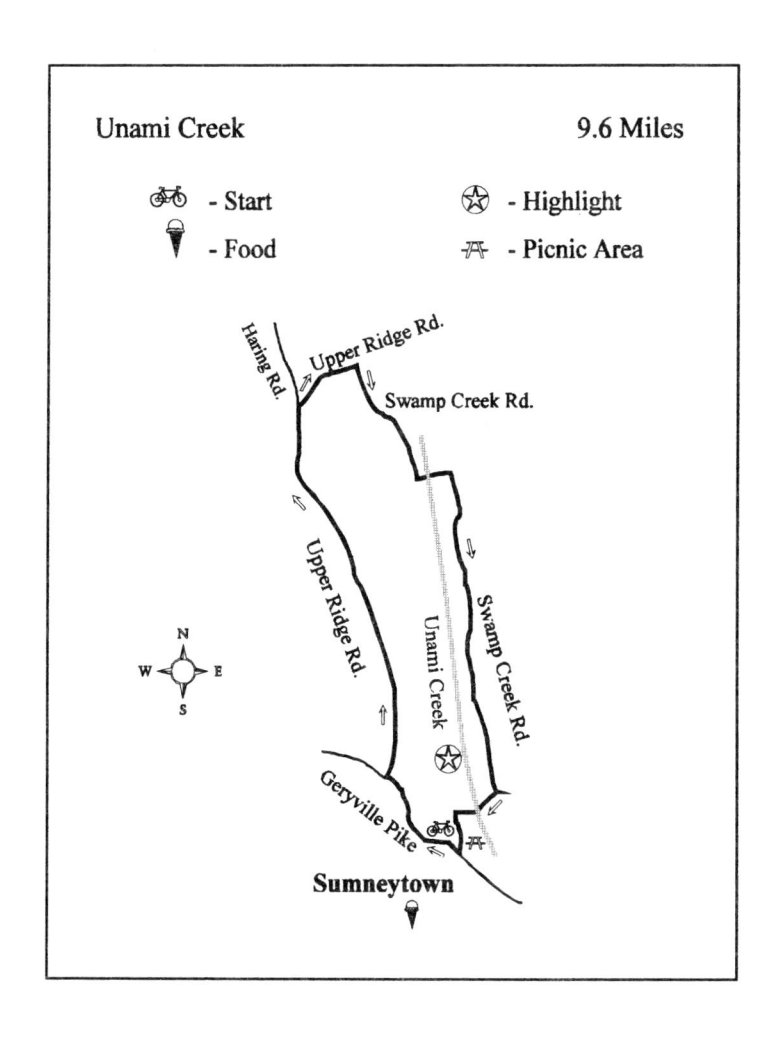

The Chocoholic Ride:
Red Hill And Trumbauersville

- 19.9 miles
- Start and finish at Green Lane Reservoir Park
- Terrain: hilly

Highlights

- Green Lane Reservoir Park
- Ann Hemyng Chocolate Factory
- Rural Montgomery and Bucks County countryside

The rolling hills along the border of Montgomery and Bucks Counties are home to more than just farms, forests, and scenic rural vistas. Tourists seldom find their way to little Trumbauersville, but those who do are rewarded with the opportunity to visit one of the best chocolate factories to be found anywhere. Ann Hemyng Candy, Inc. began in 1984 in Peddler's Village, a more well known Bucks County destination. In 1988 the company moved to Trumbauersville, where local demand resulted in the opening of a factory store. Chocolate is available here in all shapes and sizes. A new product is fudge dipped in chocolate - a chocoholic's dream! A wide assortment of other candies are also sold, and tours of the factory can be arranged for small groups. The factory closes in summer, but the store remains open.

The ride begins in Red Hill at Green Lane Reservoir Park. This large county park is popular for boating and fishing, and has picnic tables and grills available. Red Hill is a busy town with a number of stores and restaurants, but the ride quickly heads into more rural surroundings.

Food (other than chocolate) is available on the ride at Pistone Pizza and Pasta, located at the 9 mile mark in Trumbauersville. Shor's General Store, located at the 9.2 mile mark, has groceries and soft ice cream. The Finland Inn at the 12.7 mile mark serves lunch and dinner in an elegant atmosphere. For a meal before or after the ride, the Apple Dumpling Diner on Main Street in Red Hill is a popular destination.

This ride can be combined with the Unami Creek ride. From Upper Ridge Road, make a left turn onto Swamp Creek Road. Follow the directions for the Unami Creek ride, rejoining the Chocoholic Ride by making a left turn onto Finland Road from Upper Ridge Road. Remember that while this detour adds a beautiful downhill cruise along Unami Creek, it also includes a tough climb on Geryville Pike.

Getting to Green Lane Reservoir in Red Hill

From the Philadelphia area, take the Pennsylvania Turnpike or Schuylkill Expressway to King of Prussia, and take Route 422 west to the Collegeville/Phoenixville exit. From the exit, take Route 29 north to Red Hill. Just at the border between Red Hill and Pennsburg, turn left onto 11th Street and follow it for .5 miles. The entrance to Green Lane Reservoir Park (Walt Road Boat Launch Site) is on the right.

The Ride

0.0	S	Begin at the small ranger station in the park, with the ranger station on your right and ride straight out the driveway.
0.7	R	Make a right turn onto Main Street. Caution: very busy street.

0.7	L	Make an immediate left turn onto 11th Street (unmarked). You may want to walk your bicycle across Main Street because of traffic.
1.3	L	Make a left turn onto St. Paul's Church Road.
1.5	L	Make a left turn onto Frye Road.
2.2	R	Make a right turn onto Buck Road.
4.3	R	Make a right turn at the T onto Old Plain Road (unmarked).
4.8	L	Make a left turn at stop sign onto Fennel Road.
6.2	S	At intersection with Canary Road, continue straight on Fennel Road.
6.3	R	Make a right turn at the T onto Kumry Road (unmarked). Caution: there is a short, steep downhill right before the turn.
8.6	S	Go straight at stop sign onto Allentown Road. You are now in the town of Trumbauersville.
9.0	S	Ann Hemyng Chocolate Factory is on the right.
9.2	S	Pistone Pizza and Pasta is on the right.
9.3	R	Make a right turn onto West Broad Street (becomes Trumbauersville Road). Shor's General Store is on the left.
12.9	R	Make a right turn at the T in Finland onto Upper Ridge Road. (The sign says Finland Road). The Finland Inn is on the right. Upper Ridge Road climbs, sometimes steeply, for almost a mile.
13.9	R	Make a right turn onto Finland Road and enjoy a downhill cruise.
15.8	L	Make a left turn at the T onto Geryville Pike (unmarked). Caution: you are going downhill when approaching this turn.
16.5	R	Make a right turn onto West Hendricks Road.
17.2	R	Make a right turn, staying on Hendricks Road.

17.75	R	Make a right turn onto 4th Street.
17.8	L	Make an immediate left turn onto Adams Street.
18.0	R	Make a right turn onto 6th Street.
18.3	L	Make a left turn onto James Road.
18.6	L	Make a left turn onto 11th Street.
19.2	R	Make a right turn onto Main Street. Watch out for the traffic.
19.2	L	Make an immediate left turn onto 11th Street. You may want to walk your bicycle across Main Street due to heavy traffic.
19.7	R	Make a right turn into Green Lane Reservoir Park.
19.9	END	End at ranger station.

FYI

Ann Hemyng Candy, Inc., Trumbauersville (215-536-7004)
Apple Dumpling Diner, Red Hill (215-679-5000)
Finland Inn, Finland (215-679-0828)
Green Lane Reservoir Park, Green Lane (215-234-4863)
Pistone Pizza and Pasta, Trumbauersville (215-529-9553)

Bicycle Shops

Cycledrome, 38 South 8th Street, Quakertown, PA (215-536-3443)

Tailwind Bike Shop Ltd., 351 Main Street, Pennsburg, PA (215-541-4949)

Chocoholic Ride   19.9 Miles

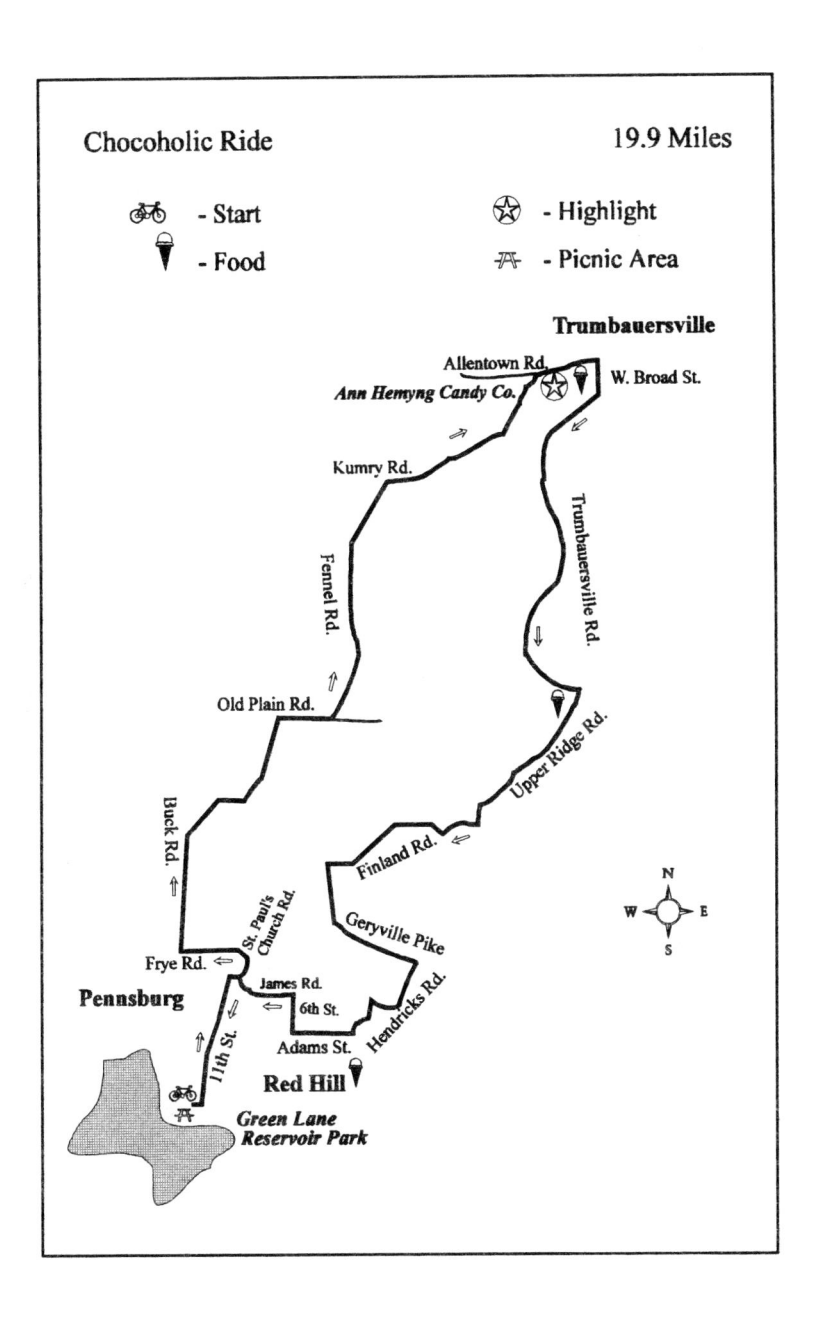

The Less Visited Bucks County

- 21.8 miles
- Start and finish at Lake Towhee Park
- Terrain: rolling

Highlights

- Lake Towhee Park
- Sheard's Mill Covered Bridge
- Nockamixon Lake State Park Environmental Study Area
- Thayer Weed Farm

The area just east of Quakertown and Sellersville is the area most easily missed by the tourists speeding off to Doylestown and New Hope. Often named "The Great Swamp" on early maps, this route contains some interesting wetlands and bird habitat. Along the route are two lakes, Towhee and Nockamixon, which are prime destinations for boaters and fishing enthusiasts. The farms are not quite as well manicured as those between New Hope and Doylestown, but are quite charming in their own right and give the area a truly rural flavor. The many hardwood forests along the route make it one of our favorite rides for viewing fall foliage.

On the right at 1.2 miles, you will see the Parkway Restaurant . Reminiscent of a 1950's style drive-in, the Parkway serves shakes, burgers, fries, etc. On numerous weekends through the warm weather, the Parkway hosts classic car shows worth stopping to see.

At 3.2 miles, you will pass the Weisel Youth Hostel on the left. Very shortly afterward, you will see some rather interesting pyramids on the right. At 10.5 miles, the Rockwild General Store is on the left. If you did not eat at the Parkway, Rockwild has very good sandwiches as well as general store fare. In fact, the atmosphere reminds us of a classic northern New England general store.

Last, but not least, pass the Thayer Weed Farm at 12.7 miles. The sign on the right is easy to miss.

Getting to Lake Towhee Park

Lake Towhee, operated by the County of Bucks, is located on Old Bethlehem Road (not to be confused with Old Bethlehem Pike on our cue sheet) between Route 563 and the tiny village of Applebachsville. From the intersection of Routes 313 and 563, go north on Route 563. After passing the Nockamixon Lake Environmental Study Center, start looking for Old Bethlehem Road on the left. Once the turn onto Old Bethlehem Road is made, Lake Towhee Park is on the right. The sign is a little hard to see while traveling in this direction. If you enter the Village of Applebachsville, you went just a bit too far.

The Ride

0.0	L	At the entrance to Lake Towhee Park, make a left turn onto Old Bethlehem Road
1.2	R	Make a right turn onto West Thatcher Road. The Parkway is on the corner.
1.7	L	Make a left turn onto Covered Bridge Road. .3 miles later, go through the Sheard's Mill Covered Bridge. The Tohicken Campground is on the left, just after the bridge.
2.55	L	Make a left turn at the T onto Richlandtown Road (**unmarked**).

3.8	L	Make a left turn onto Sterner Mill Road
3.85	R	Make a right turn onto Route 563 (unmarked). This road can be busy, but it has a nice shoulder. Immediately pass Nockamixon Lake State Park Environmental Study Area on left.
4.8	L	Make a left turn onto Route 313. Use caution. This is a busy intersection.
5.0	R	Make a right turn onto West Rock Road. It is the first right turn after entering Route 313. We do not want you to miss it. Route 313 is not fun to ride on.
6.5	R	After descending a short hill (pretty pond on left), make a right turn at the T onto Three Mile Run Road (unmarked).
8.6	R	Make a right turn onto Park Avenue. This becomes Old Bethlehem Pike (not to be confused with Old Bethlehem Road). Rockwild will be on the left at 10.5 miles.
11.1	R	Make a right turn onto Paletown Road. Just before Paletown Road, you will see BARC Production Services on the left. Paletown Road is easy to miss, as you are gaining speed down a short hill. Weekdays, one of your authors works at BARC. Feel free to stop for water, or just to say hi!
12.1	R	Make a right turn onto Smoketown Road. The Commonwealth Flag Company is on the left. Smoketown Road becomes Muskrat Road. Pass the Thayer Weed Farm on the right at 12.7 miles.
13.1	L	Make a left turn onto Rich Hill Road, just after passing the state game lands on the left. This road becomes Rock Hill Road.
15.4	S	Cross Route 313. This is a busy intersection. Rock Hill Road becomes Ax Handle Road.
15.8	BL	Bear left, staying on Ax Handle Road.

16.6	R	Make a right turn onto Thatcher Road, immediately crossing a bridge over Morgan Creek.
17.8	L	Make a left turn onto Union Road. A signpost on the right will say "Richlandtown Road'" while a signpost on the left will say "Union Road."
18.65	R	Make a right turn onto Apple Road
19.4	R	Make a right turn onto Woodland Drive. You will see a sign straight ahead saying "Beck Road." After making the turn you should see a sign saying "Haycock Twp."
19.9	BL	Bear left onto Creamery Road.
20.2	BL	Bear left. Creamery Road becomes Apple Road, even later becoming Applebachsville Road.
21.35	R	Inside the tiny village of Applebachsville, make a right turn onto Old Bethlehem Road.
21.8	END	End at Lake Towhee Park on the left.

FYI

Lake Towhee Park, Applebachsville (215-757-0571)
Parkway Drive In Restaurant, Quakertown (215-538-2904)
Rockwild General Store, Sellersville (215-257-7627)

Bicycle Shops

Bike Line, Main & Old Dublin, Doylestown, PA (215-348-8015)

Cycledrome, 38 South 8th Street, Quakertown, PA (215-536-3443)

Cycle Sports LTD., 641 North Main Street, Doylestown, PA (215-340-2526)

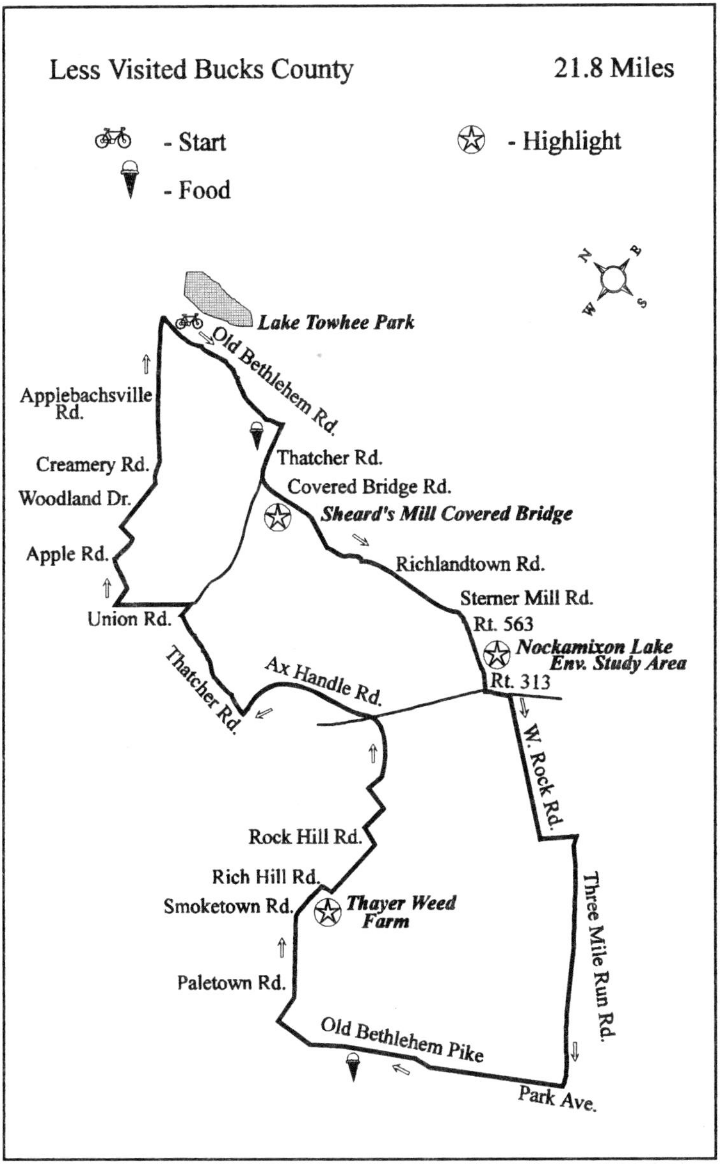
Less Visited Bucks County
21.8 Miles
- Start
- Highlight
- Food
N
E
S
W
Lake Towhee Park
Old Bethlehem Rd.
Applebachsville Rd.
Creamery Rd.
Woodland Dr.
Apple Rd.
Union Rd.
Thatcher Rd.
Covered Bridge Rd.
Sheard's Mill Covered Bridge
Richlandtown Rd.
Sterner Mill Rd.
Rt. 563
Nockamixon Lake Env. Study Area
Rt. 313
Thatcher Rd.
Ax Handle Rd.
W. Rock Rd.
Rock Hill Rd.
Rich Hill Rd.
Smoketown Rd.
Thayer Weed Farm
Paletown Rd.
Three Mile Run Rd.
Old Bethlehem Pike
Park Ave.

Nockamixon's East Shore

- 20.5 miles
- Start and end ride at the Three Mile Run Boat Access within Nockamixon Lake State Park
- Terrain: rolling

Highlights

- Nockamixon Lake State Park
- Bucks County farm country

The area just east of Nockamixon Lake contains some of the most scenic farm country in Bucks County. However, it is still a little to the west of the heavy traffic found in the New Hope-Doylestown corridor. Nockamixon Lake itself is quite beautiful and attracts scores of boaters and fishing enthusiasts each year.

There are no stores for food purchases along this route. However, the waterfalls noted at the 5.8 mile mark might be a pretty place to eat a carry-along picnic.

Getting to Three Mile Run Boat Access

Coming from Doylestown on Route 313 north, look for Three Mile Run Road on the right, just past the traffic light at Route 563. A brown and white sign indicating a turn for the "Region Office - State Parks" is another clue to start looking for Three Mile Run Road. Turn right onto Three Mile Run Road from Route 313. The Boat Access is about a mile up the road on the left.

The Ride

0.0	L	From the Three Mile Run Boat Access driveway, make a left turn onto Three Mile Run Road.
0.3	R	Make a right turn at the stop sign onto an unmarked road.
0.4	S	Straight onto Elephant Road.
0.5	BL	Bear left onto Creek Road West.
1.2	L	Make a left turn onto Ridge Road
2.3	BL	Bear left, staying on Ridge Road. Ridge becomes South Park Road.
5.8	S	View scenic waterfalls on left!
6.7	R	Make a right turn onto Park Road.
6.8	R	Make a right turn at the Yield sign
7.2	R	Make a right turn onto Creamery Road.
7.6	S	Straight onto Fretz Valley Road.
8.3	L	Make a left turn onto Deer Run Road.
8.9	R	Make a right turn onto Farm School Road.
10.2	R	Make a right turn at the T onto Keller's Church Road (unmarked).
11.6	L	Make a left turn onto Edge Hill Road. Use caution, as oncoming cars will be coming over the crest of a hill.
12.1	L	Make a left turn at the T onto Birch Lane (unmarked).

12.6	R	Make a right turn at the T onto Sweet Briar Road (unmarked).
14.4	L	Make a left turn at the T onto Elephant Road (unmarked).
16.0	R	Make a right turn onto Blue School Road (a sign says "Day Dream Farms").
16.7	R	Make a right turn onto Bucks Road (at time of this writing, the sign was partially damaged).
17.8	R	Make a right turn at the T onto Sweet Briar Road (unmarked).
18.1	L	Make a left turn onto Bucks Road. Begin a steep ascent of a hill.
18.8	L	Make a left turn at the T onto Ridge Road (unmarked).
19.3	R	Make a right turn onto Butler Lane.
19.9	R	Make a right turn onto Three Mile Run Road.
20.5	END	End at the Three Mile Run Boat Access.

FYI

Nockamixon Lake State Park, Quakertown (215-529-7300)

Bicycle Shops

Bike Line, Main & Old Dublin, Doylestown, PA (215-348-8015)

Cycledrome, 38 South 8th Street, Quakertown, PA (215-536-3443)

Cycle Sports LTD., 641 North Main Street, Doylestown, PA (215-340-2526)

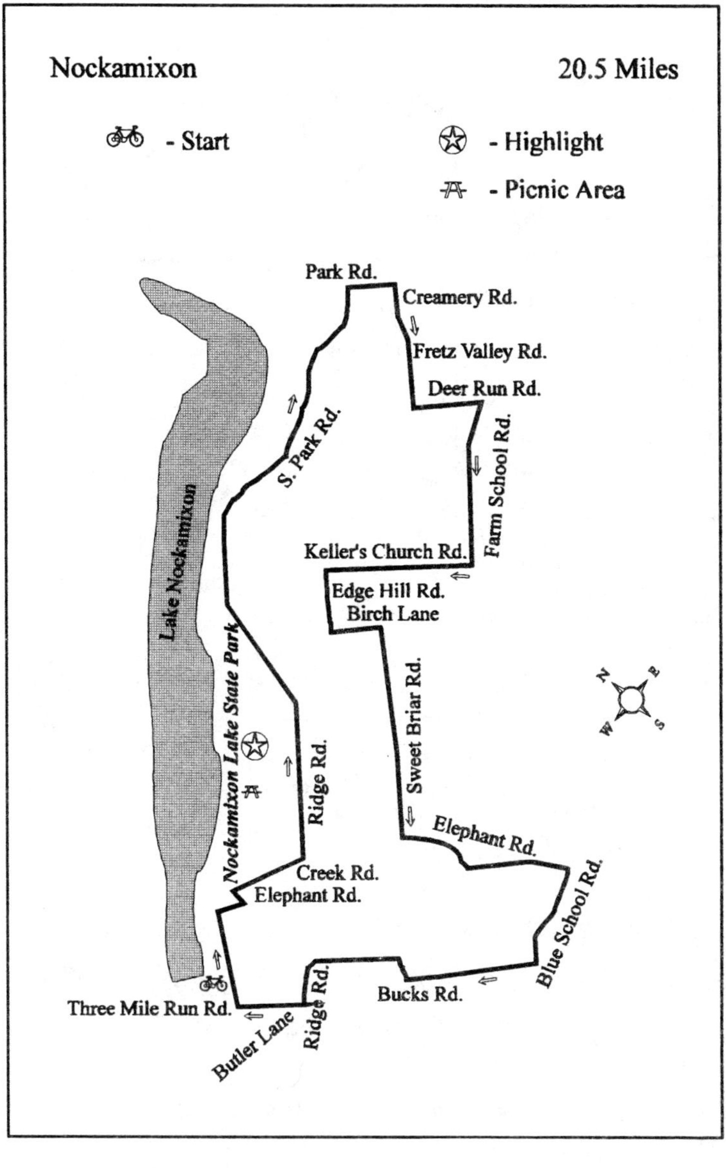
Nockamixon
20.5 Miles
- Start
- Highlight
- Picnic Area
Park Rd.
Creamery Rd.
Fretz Valley Rd.
Deer Run Rd.
S. Park Rd.
Farm School Rd.
Lake Nockamixon
Keller's Church Rd.
Edge Hill Rd.
Birch Lane
Nockamixon Lake State Park
Sweet Briar Rd.
N
E
W
S
Ridge Rd.
Elephant Rd.
Creek Rd.
Elephant Rd.
Blue School Rd.
Three Mile Run Rd.
Bucks Rd.
Ridge Rd.
Butler Lane

Rocks And Woods: Ringing Rocks Park, Erwinna And Revere

- 25.25 miles
- Start and end at Ringing Rocks Park, just west of Upper Black Eddy
- Terrain: challenging hills

Highlights

- Ringing Rocks Park
- Pretty wooded streams
- Two covered bridges

The area between Lake Nockamixon and the Delaware River is sometimes known as the Palisades Region of Bucks County. Traveling in a northeast direction from Lake Nockamixon, the hills get higher and higher before making a very pronounced drop just before the Delaware River. The result is some very challenging yet beautiful country roads for the cyclist.

The ride begins at Ringing Rocks County Park. The sixty-five acre tract got its name from a boulder field inside the park. Visitors enjoy bringing hammers to the boulder field and listening to the rocks "ring" when tapped. Another fine feature of the park is a small, but beautiful waterfall less than a mile from the boulder field. A hiking trail connects both the boulder field and the waterfall with the parking lot where the ride starts. If time and energy level permit, the short hike is a very nice post-ride activity.

While the ride features many beautiful farms and country homes, much of it travels through thick forests crisscrossed by numerous little streams. Twice on the ride, these streams are crossed by quaint nineteenth century covered bridges that enhance the rural ambiance.

Food is available on the ride at The Top of the Mall Deli, reached by continuing on Beaver Run Road at the 20.7 mile point. The deli is located at the intersection of Beaver Run Road with Route 611. There is a picnic area by the parking lot in Ringing Rocks Park.

It should be noted that we experienced a significant amount of loose gravel and potholes on many of the roads on this ride. However, even on skinny tires, we experienced no real difficulties as long as we rode slowly through the rougher sections. The beauty of the forests and streams makes up for the minor inconveniences.

Getting to Ringing Rocks Park

Ringing Rocks Park is near Upper Black Eddy, located on the Delaware River. From Philadelphia, take Route 95 north to Route 32, and follow Route 32 (River Road) north through New Hope and on up to Upper Black Eddy. Just past the Bridgeton House Bed and Breakfast, turn left onto Bridgeton Hill Road. Go 1.5 miles and turn right onto Ringing Rocks Road.

Alternately, take Route 611 north from Doylestown. Shortly after passing Schoolhouse Apartments, in the tiny town of Revere, Route 611 bears left and you continue straight onto Beaver Run Road. Turn left onto Marienstein Road, continue 3.8 miles, and turn left onto Ringing Rocks Road.

The Ride

0.0	L	From the parking lot at Ringing Rocks County Park, turn left onto Ringing Rocks Road.
0.2	L	Make a left turn at the T onto Bridgeton Hill Road (unmarked).
0.7	R	Make a right turn onto Chestnut Ridge Road (sign for Chestnut Ridge is on the left). The road soon becomes Upper Tinicum Church Road.
3.1	L	Make a left turn onto Union School Road. Caution: loose gravel!
3.2	BR	Bear right onto Upper Tinicum Church Road.
3.6	BR	Bear right, staying on Upper Tinicum Church Road.
3.9	L	Make a left turn at the T onto Perry Auger Road. The road soon becomes Upper Tinicum Church Road again.
5.5	L	Make a left turn onto Geigel Hill Road.
5.8	S	Go through Erwinna Covered Bridge.
6.0	R	Make a right turn onto Headquarters Road (just before the Erwinna Post Office).
6.9	BR	Bear right onto Tinicum Creek Road.
7.0	L	Make a left turn onto Hollow Horn Road.
8.25	L	Make a left turn at the T, staying on Hollow Horn Road (unmarked).
8.5	S	Go through the Frankenfield Covered Bridge and continue straight, staying on Hollow Horn Road.
10.6	S	Go straight onto Red Hill Road (Hollow Horn Road turns left).
11.7	R	Turn right onto Headquarters Road.
11.8	R	Turn right, staying on Headquarters Road.
12.35	R	Turn right, staying on Headquarters Road.

14.1	L	Make a left turn onto Cafferty Road.
15.35	L	Make a left turn onto Geigel Hill/Cafferty Road.
15.45	R	Make a right turn onto Cafferty Road.
16.2	S	Go straight at the stop sign.
16.95	L	Turn left onto Tammany Road. Tammany Road becomes Strocks Grove Road.
18.1	L	Turn left onto Rock Ridge Road.
19.0	R	Turn right onto Byers Road.
19.65	R	Turn right onto Beaver Run Road.
20.7	R	Turn right onto Marienstein Road. (For a short side trip for food, continue .4 mile on Beaver Run Road to the Top of the Mall Deli at the intersection with Route 611. Caution: busy road.
22.05	R	Turn right onto Lonely Cottage Road.
23.1	BR	Bear right, staying on Lonely Cottage Road.
24.2	BL	Bear left, staying on Lonely Cottage Road.
24.6	S	Go straight at the stop sign.
25.2	R	Turn right onto Ringing Rocks Road.
25.3	END	End ride by turning left into Ringing Rocks County Park.

FYI

Ringing Rocks Park, Upper Black Eddy (215-757-0571)

Bicycle Shops

Bike Line, 25th Street Shopping Center, Easton, PA (610-253-8103)

Freeman's Bicycle Shop, 52 Bridge Street, Frenchtown, NJ (908-996-7712)

97

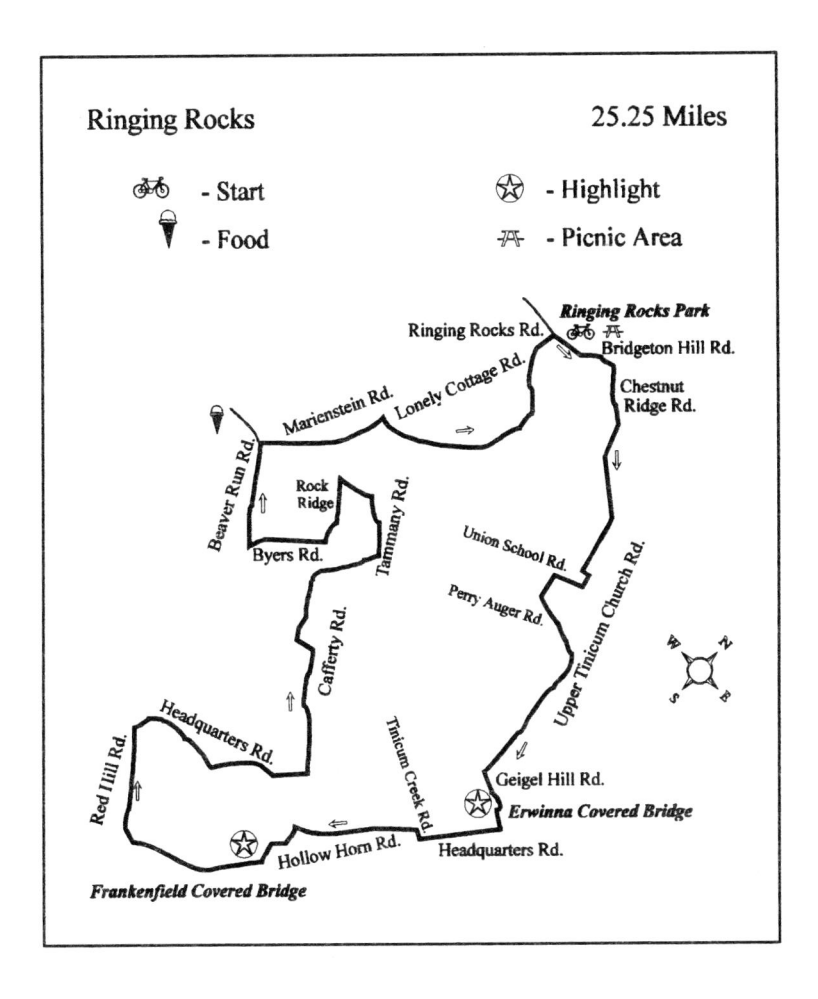

The Peace Valley Ride

- 11.9 miles
- Start and end at the Peace Valley Nature Center
- Terrain: flat to rolling with one steep ascent.

Highlights

- Peace Valley Nature Center
- Peace Valley Park
- Peace Valley Winery
- The Pearl S. Buck House

After living halfway around the world, writer Pearl Buck chose the tranquil farmlands of central Bucks County area for her home. This route gives the rider the flavor of the countryside surrounding Buck's home. It begins at the Peace Valley Nature Center, a beautiful wildlife preserve located at the northeast end of Lake Galena. Since the ride itself is less than 12 miles, plenty of time can be spent exploring the nature center's 14 mile hiking trail system before or after the tour.

The beginning of the ride makes use of a "bike and hike" path that surrounds most of the lake. Although it is free of motor vehicles, the path contains numerous pedestrians, especially dog walkers. Therefore slower speeds are the rule and caution is advised. However, the path runs very close to the shoreline and is home to some of the prettiest lakefront riding in the region.

The Peace Valley Winery can be found at the 5.6 mile mark. Two dozen varieties of grapes are grown on 20 acres of land for the winery. A shop and tasting room are located on the premises.

The Pearl Buck House is located at the 8.8 mile mark. Built in 1835, the house is a fine example of early rural Pennsylvania architecture. Its interior reflects the famous author's fascination with both Asia and early America. For instance, two Pennsylvania jugs sit on top of the beautifully carved Chinese Hardwood desk at which Buck wrote her famous novel, "The Good Earth."

Food can be purchased in season at the Tabora Farm and Orchard Store, located at 5.8 miles. Another option is the Penn View Farm Store, specializing in baked goods and diary products, at the 9.5 mile mark.

Getting to the Peace Valley Nature Center

The center is located at 170 Chapman Road. From Doylestown, go northwest on Rt. 313 to New Galena Road, (Ginger Bread Square on the corner). Make a left turn onto New Galena Road. From New Galena Road, turn left onto Chapman Road. The parking lot for the nature center will be on the left.

The Ride

0.0	L	From the parking lot at Peace Valley Nature Center (facing the Nature Center buildings), make a left turn onto Chapman Road.
0.2	R	After crossing the bridge, make a right turn onto the bike and hike path.
1.2	S	Go straight. The bike and hike path becomes Creek Road.
1.4	S	Go straight. Cross Old Limekiln Road.
2.15	R	Make a right turn into Peace Valley Park at the Galena Village Entrance (2nd entrance).

2.25	L	Make a left turn onto the bike and hike path, just before the waterfront. Immediately cross a small brown bridge.
3.0	R	Staying on the bike and hike path, make a right turn, crossing the dam to the opposite shore of the lake.
3.4	BR	Bear right, staying on the bike and hike path.
4.65	S	A yellow pole marks the end of the bike and hike path. Continue straight, merging with the driveway (New Galena Road) coming in from the left.
4.8	L	Make a left turn at the T onto Old Limekiln Road (unmarked). A green sign says "winery." Begin ascending a long hill.
5.3	S	Go straight. Cross King Road.
5.6	S	The Peace Valley Winery is on the left.
5.8	L	Make a left turn onto Upper Stump Road.
6.2	R	Make a right turn onto Upper Church Road. Tabora Farm and Orchard Store is on the right, just before the turn.
6.7	R	Make a right turn onto Broad Street.
7.3	L	Make a left turn onto Welcome House Road. The sign is on the left and may be partially obscured by foliage. The road is named after an international adoption agency founded by Pearl S. Buck.
8.2	R	Make a right turn onto Dublin Road.
8.5	S	Go straight. The Pearl Buck House is on the left.
8.6	R	Make a right turn onto Bypass Road (unmarked). It is the first right turn after passing the Pearl Buck House.
9.2	R	Turn right onto Middle Road.
9.5	S	Go straight. Penn View Farms is on the left.

10.0	L	Turn left onto Upper Stump Road.
10.4	R	Turn right onto Keller Road.
11.0	L	Turn left at the T onto King Road (unmarked).
11.2	R	Turn right onto Chapman Road. Begin a sharp descent into the valley. Caution: stop sign at the bottom of the hill.
11.6	S	Go straight, crossing New Galena Road. Continue sharp descent.
11.9	END	End the ride at Peace Valley Nature Center.

FYI

Peace Valley Nature Center, New Britain (215-345-7860)
Peace Valley Park, New Britain (215-757-0571)
Peace Valley Winery, Chalfont (215-249-9058)
Pearl S. Buck House, Perkasie (215-249-0100)
Penn View Farm Store, Chalfont (215-249-9128)
Tabora Farm and Orchard Store, Chalfont (215-249-3016)

Bicycle Shops

Bike Line, Main & Old Dublin, Doylestown, PA (215-348-8015)

Bike Line, Route 202 & 309 & 463, Montgomeryville, PA (215-361-7900)

Cycle Sports LTD., 641 North Main Street, Doylestown, PA (215-340-2526)

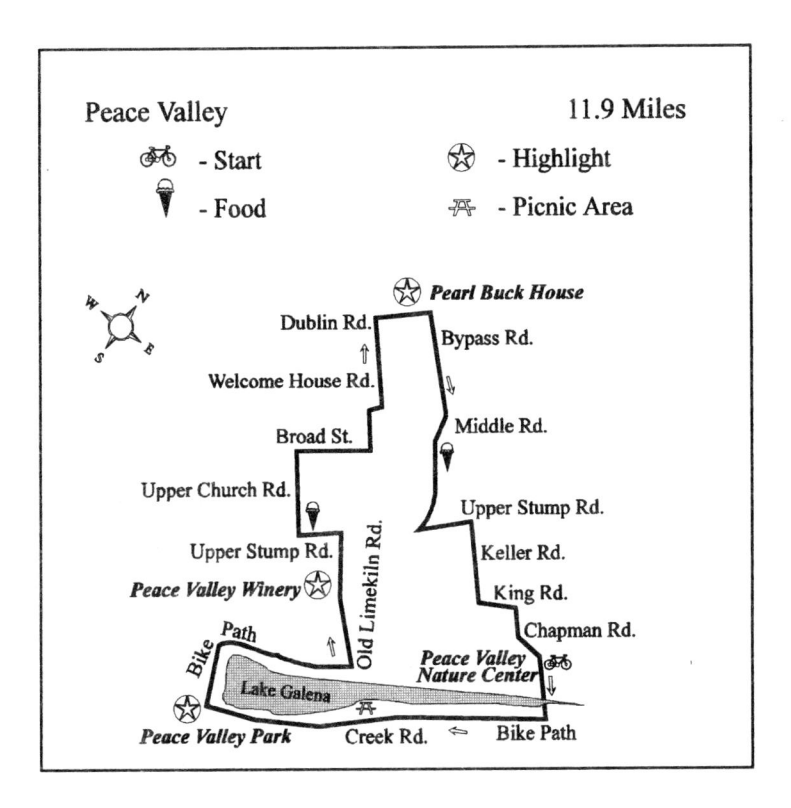

Peace Valley

11.9 Miles

- 🚲 - Start
- 🍦 - Food
- ★ - Highlight
- ⛺ - Picnic Area

★ *Pearl Buck House*
Dublin Rd.
Bypass Rd.
Welcome House Rd.
Middle Rd.
Broad St.
Upper Church Rd.
Upper Stump Rd.
Upper Stump Rd.
Keller Rd.
Peace Valley Winery ★
Old Limekiln Rd.
King Rd.
Chapman Rd.
Bike Path
Peace Valley Nature Center
Lake Galena
★ *Peace Valley Park*
Creek Rd.
Bike Path

America In Miniature: Roadside America And Shartlesville

- 20.8 miles
- Start and end at Roadside America, Shartlesville
- Terrain: rolling

HIGHLIGHTS

- Roadside America
- Antiques and crafts stores
- Haag's Hotel
- Beautiful Irish Creek

Founded in 1765, Shartlesville is located on the northern edge of Berks County's farmlands. Just a little outside the center of the village is Roadside America, advertised as the "largest known miniature village." With 300 miniature buildings and 2,250 feet of train and trolley tracks, Roadside America attracts visitors from all over the world.

If model trains and miniature buildings attract people to Roadside America, antiques and Pennsylvania Dutch cooking are what attracts people to Shartlesville itself. Famous for the latter is Haag's Hotel. The Haag/Seitzinger family has been serving Pennsylvania Dutch foods for five generations, occupying the current building since 1915. The hotel's specialty is all you can eat, family-style dinners, using traditional Pennsylvania Dutch recipes and including fifteen or more side dishes! In season, all fresh fruits and vegetables come from adjoining neighborhood farms. Dairy products, as well as the tasty apple butter, are also locally produced. Delicious and inexpensive breakfasts and lunches are also served.

Getting to Shartlesville

From the Philadelphia area, take Route 422 west to Reading. In Reading, leave Route 422, getting on Route 183. Just beyond the village of Bernville, make a right turn onto Shartlesville Road and follow it to Shartlesville. Once inside the town, make a left turn onto Olde Route 22 to get to Roadside America.

The Ride

0.0	R	Begin the ride in the parking lot in front of Roadside America. Turn right into the driveway between Roadside America and the Pennsylvania Dutch Gift Haus (just before the statue of the Amish people)
0.1	L	Make a left turn onto Olde 22.
1.2	R	After traveling through downtown Shartlesville, make a right turn onto Schoolhouse Road.
2.7	L	Make a left turn at the stop sign onto Skyline Drive.
3.3	S	Go straight at the yield sign, staying on Skyline Drive.
4.4	S	Go straight. Skyline Drive becomes Lesher's Mill Road.
5.3	L	Make a left turn at the T onto Tilden Road.
5.7	S	Go straight at the stop sign, staying on Tilden Road.
6.7	R	Make a right turn onto Berne Road.

8.1	R	Make a right turn, staying on Berne Road. The sign on the left says "North End Road."
8.4	S	Go straight at the stop sign, entering the village of Centerport.
8.6	R	Turn right onto Irish Creek Road.
10.4	BR	Bear right, staying on Irish Creek Road.
13.4	BR	Bear right at the yield sign, staying on Irish Creek Road.
15.4	R	Turn right onto Shartlesville Road.
16.0	L	Turn left onto Manbeck Road. Use caution when making this turn.
17.9	S	Go straight at the stop sign, staying on Manbeck Road.
18.8	R	Make a right turn onto Spring Road. Spring Road becomes Tulpehocken Road.
20.0	R	Make a right turn onto Olde 22.
20.7	L	Make a left turn into Roadside America.
20.8	END	End the ride in front of Roadside America.

FYI

Haag's Hotel, Shartlesville (610-488-6692)
Roadside America, Shartlesville (610-488-6241)

Bicycle Shop

Spokes Bike Shop, Route 61, Hamburg, PA (610-562-8900)

Shartlesville

20.8 Miles

- 🚲 - Start
- 🍦 - Food
- ✪ - Highlight

Centerport

Berne Rd.

Irish Creek Rd.

Tilden Rd.

Irish Creek

Lesher's Mill Rd.

Skyline Dr.

Schoolhouse Rd.

Roadside America ✪ 🚲🍦 **Shartlesville**

Shartlesville Rd.

Olde 22

Manbeck Rd.

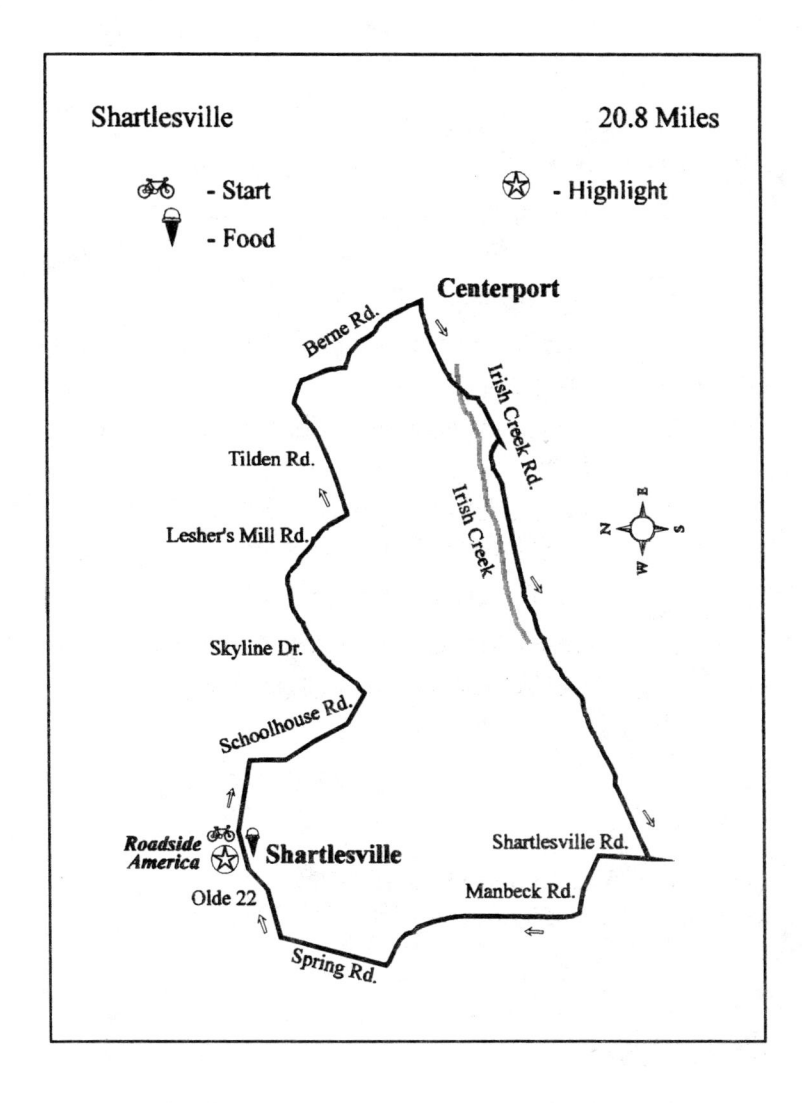

Spring Rd.

Rails And Sails:
Leaser Lake and Kempton

- 31.3 miles (36.5 miles with optional side trip to Hawk Mountain or 32.2 miles with optional side trip to Leaser Lake)
- Start and finish at the W.K.& S. Steam Railroad in Kempton
- Terrain: rolling with a few steep climbs

Highlights

- W.K.& S. Steam Railroad
- Hawk Mountain
- Leaser Lake
- Mountain scenery

This route provides an excellent opportunity to explore the beautiful farmlands along the base of the Blue Mountain. The region is probably most famous for the wildlife sanctuary, created by environmentalists in the 1930s, on top of Hawk Mountain. The unique air currents make Hawk Mountain's rocky lookout one of the most ideal spots to view the annual hawk migrations. During the height of the autumn season, visitors come for all over the world to enjoy the hawks, as well as the spectacular scenery.

The main route of the ride is mostly rolling hills with only a few short steep climbs. However, the optional side trip up Hawk Mountain is the most difficult climb in this book, if not the most difficult climb in southeastern Pennsylvania! In 1989, the climb also gained the attention of cycling enthusiasts when it was included as part of a stage in the Tour de Trump.

A much less ambitious undertaking is the optional side trip to Leaser Lake. The lake is small as bodies of water go, although large enough for sailing and fishing, and is a very pretty place to enjoy a break and perhaps a picnic lunch.

Another attraction of interest is the W.K. & S. Steam Railroad, located at the starting point. During the summer, rail fans can enjoy an old fashioned train ride alongside Ontelaunee Creek.

There are no restaurants along the route, although the tiny village of New Tripoli has a bar prominently located in the center of town. At 11.85 miles, the village of Wanamakers contains a general store with a very nice selection of dried fruits, nut mixes and homemade baked goods. The Kempton Hotel is another option for a meal before or after the ride.

Getting to Kempton

From the Philadelphia area, take either Route 309 north or the northeast extension of the PA turnpike to Route 78 west. At the Lenhartsville exit take Route 143 north. Turn right onto Route 737 and follow the road into Kempton. Turn onto Creek Road just past the Kempton Hotel, following the signs for the W.K.& S. Railroad.

The Ride

0.0	S	From the parking lot of the W.K. & S. Railroad, with the trains on your right, go straight out the Community Center Drive.
0.1	S	Straight at the stop sign.
0.15	R	Make a right turn at the second stop sign. The sign says "Kistler Valley Road."
0.25	R	Make a right turn onto Route 737.

0.7	L	Make a left turn onto Route 143.
1.1	R	Make a right turn onto Hawk Mountain Road. Look for sign saying "Hawk Mountain Bird Sanctuary." A prominent rock outcropping called the Pinnacle can be viewed on the left while traveling this road.
5.2	R	Make a right turn onto Mountain Road.
		Optional side trip to Hawk Mountain Sanctuary: To get to the Hawk Mountain Sanctuary, continue on Hawk Mountain Road instead of making this turn. Follow Hawk Mountain Road 2.6 miles to the sanctuary. This road could be busy during the autumn season. To rejoin the ride, simply turn around and ride back to the intersection of Hawk Mountain Road and Mountain road. (Be very careful descending the mountain). Turn left onto Mountain Road.
8.5	L	Make a left turn onto Quaker City Road. The sign is on the left and easy to miss.
9.9	S	Continue straight. Quaker City Road becomes Slateville Road.
10.9		**Optional side trip to Leaser Lake:** To get to Leaser Lake, turn left here onto Utt Road. Continue for .5 mile and turn left onto Leaser Road. In .1 mile, turn right at the sign pointing to Leaser Lake and ride .3 mile farther to the lake. To return to the bike ride, retrace your way back to Slateville Road and turn left.
11.3	L	Make a left turn onto Route 143. Watch for Wanamakers General Store.
11.9	R	Make a right turn onto Allemaengel Road.
12.4	S	Continue straight, staying on Allemaengel Road.
13.2	BL	Bear left, staying on Allemaengel Road.
13.7	BL	Bear left, staying on Allemaengel Road.

14.0	R	Turn right, staying on Allemaengel Road.
16.6	S	Straight at stop sign in New Tripoli onto Decator Street.
17.2	R	Make a right turn onto Washington Street, at the end of town.
17.3	S	Go straight at the stop sign. Washington Street becomes Camp Meeting Road.
18.4	L	Make a left turn onto Flint Hill Road.
20.7	R	Make a right turn onto Werley's Corner Road.
23.5	R	Make a right turn onto Holben's Valley Road.
25.5	S	Go straight. Holben's Valley Road becomes Kistler Valley Road.
31.1	R	Make a right turn onto Creek Road.
31.2	BR	Bear right onto Community Drive.
31.3	END	End ride at W.K & S. Railroad.

FYI

Hawk Mountain, Kempton (610-756-6961)
Kempton Hotel, Kempton (610-756-6588)
W.K. & S. Railroad, Kempton (610-756-6469)
Wanamakers General Store, Wanamakers (610-756-6558)

Bicycle Shops

Bicycle Den, 226 West Main Street, Kutztown, PA (610-683-5566)

Bike Line, 1728 Tilghman Street, Allentown, PA (610-439-1724)

Bike Line, 831 Chestnut Street, Emmaus, PA (610-967-1029)

Spokes Bike Shop, Route 61, Hamburg, PA (610-562-8900)

Kempton

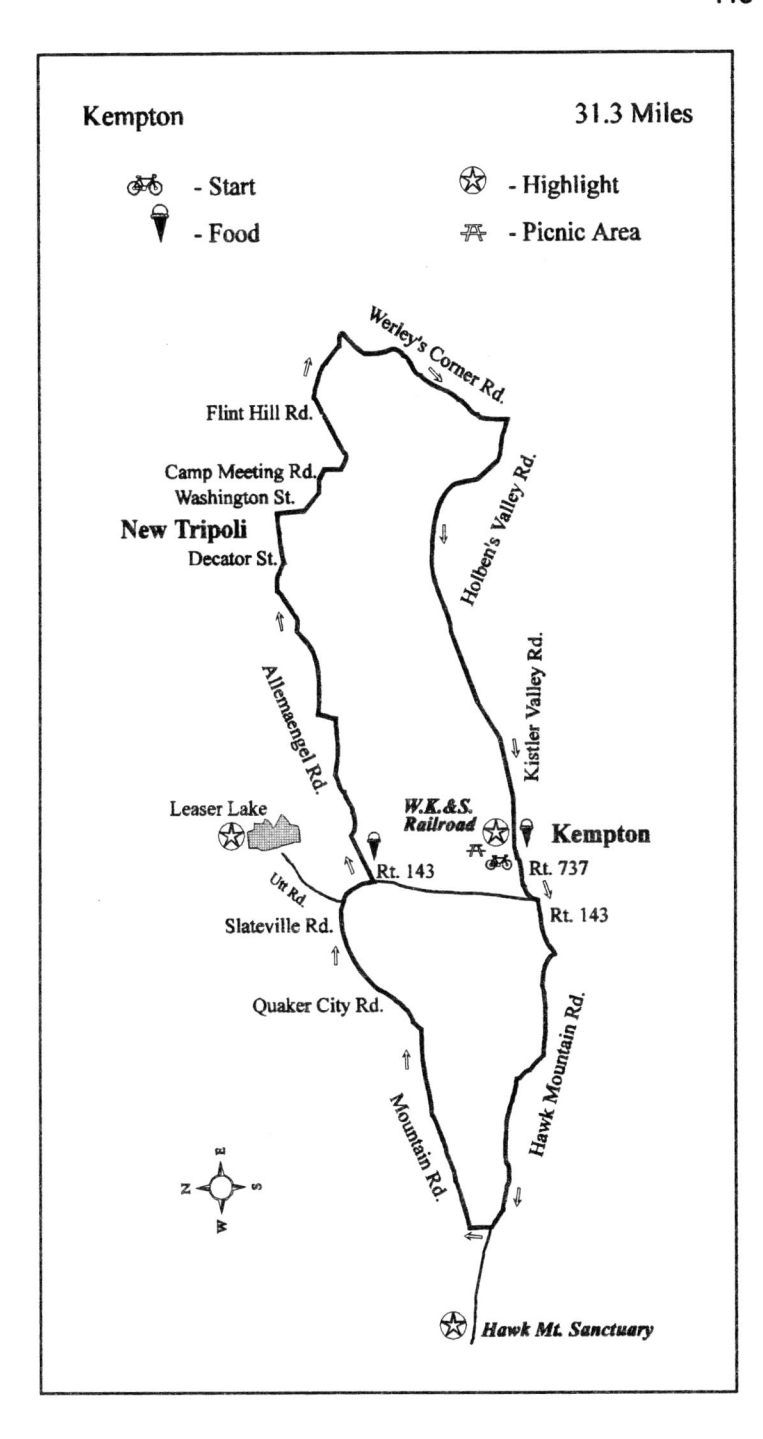

31.3 Miles

- 🚲 - Start
- 🍦 - Food
- ⭐ - Highlight
- 🪑 - Picnic Area

Werley's Corner Rd.
Flint Hill Rd.
Camp Meeting Rd.
Washington St.
New Tripoli
Decator St.
Holben's Valley Rd.
Kistler Valley Rd.
Allemaengel Rd.
Leaser Lake
W.K.&S. Railroad
Kempton
Utt Rd.
Rt. 143
Rt. 737
Slateville Rd.
Rt. 143
Quaker City Rd.
Mountain Rd.
Hawk Mountain Rd.
Hawk Mt. Sanctuary

113

Following The Tire Tracks of LeMond: Orwigsburg and Hawk Mountain

- 17.5 miles
- Start and finish at the Orwigsburg Community Parking Center
- Terrain: rolling

Highlights

- Historic Orwigsburg
- Pennsylvania Dutch countryside
- Views of renowned Hawk Mountain

Twice the southern portion of Schuylkill County played host to the world's greatest cyclists, including Greg LeMond. At one point in its colorful history, the area also hosted "The Greatest." In the early 1970s, heavyweight champ Muhammad Ali built a training facility just across Route 61 from Deer Lake.

The ride begins in Orwigsburg, a one-time host to the Tour Du Pont and now home to many antique and craft shops. The route quickly moves into some very rural country. Many of the roads are unnamed on local maps and unmarked along the ride, and a bicycle computer is practically a necessity in order to follow the route. At numerous points throughout the ride, outstanding views of famous Hawk Mountain are afforded. During the first quarter of this century, Hawk Mountain was a popular place to hunt birds of prey. However, for over fifty years, the summit of the mountain has been preserved as a sanctuary, attracting visitors from all over the world.

Food is available in Orwigsburg at a number of pizza and sandwich shops. Tasty ice cream, hot dogs, and nachos can be purchased at Maple Leaf Farm, located at the 6.2 mile mark.

Combining cycling with hiking on the Appalachian Trail or antique shopping in Orwigsburg could fill a whole weekend. Right along the route is Serenity Farm, featuring a "milk house" that was converted into a single unit lodging facility overlooking the farm's pond. Owners Felix and Sherry Bartush renovated the structure to create a unique living and dining area, a modern kitchen and a second story sleeping loft. Future plans include converting part of the farmhouse into a country inn. Serenity Farm and Milk House is located on Reddale Road, 1.8 miles east of Orwigsburg.

Getting to Orwigsburg

From the Philadelphia area, take Route 422 to Reading. In Reading, leave Route 422 to enter Route 61 north. Just past the village of Deer Lake, look for a sign to the right pointing to Orwigsburg. Follow that road into town. Once in town, the road becomes Market Street. In the center of town is a very pretty square. The community parking lot is located on the right side of the square at Warren Street.

The Ride

0.0	R	From the Orwigsburg Community Parking Center (at the corner of Market and Warren Streets), make a right turn onto Market Street. Enjoy a long downhill through the center of town.
0.4	R	At the Orwigsburg Post Office, make a right turn onto Lincoln Avenue.

1.0	R	Make a right turn onto an unmarked road. A sign on a pole says "Ruff's Nursery."
2.55	BL	Bear left and enjoy a nice gradual downhill.
3.8	R	After passing the Swiss Chalet Restaurant, make a right turn at the T (unmarked).
4.2	S	Go straight, crossing Route 443.
4.6	L	Make a left turn onto an unmarked road. Pass a green house on the right after making the turn.
4.95	R	Make a right turn onto Frisbee Road. Descend a half-mile hill. Watch the curves!
5.6	R	Make a right turn onto Reddale Road (unmarked). A red garage is on the right.
5.9	L	Make a left turn onto an unmarked road. Watch for a sign for Maple Leaf Farm.
6.2	S	Maple Leaf Farm is on the right.
6.25	L	Make a left turn at the T onto Pine Creek Road. A white church is on the right just before making the turn. Local cyclists have reported to us that they have observed cars running the stop sign. Please use caution!
7.3	L	Make a left turn onto Pheasant Run Road.
7.6	R	Make a right turn onto Lake Front Drive (unmarked).
8.4	R	Make a right turn at the stop sign (unmarked).
8.8	S	Straight on Lake Front Drive.
9.0	L	After viewing the lake on the right, make a left turn onto Spruce Road.
9.35	R	Make a right at the T. Begin ascending a hill.
9.95	L	Make a left turn at the intersection at the top of the hill (unmarked). A sign ahead says "Pavement Ends, 550 feet." Enjoy a mile long downhill, but watch the curves!

11.1	L	At the bottom of the hill, make a left turn at the T (unmarked).
11.85	R	Make a right turn onto Pheasant Run Road (unmarked) at the four way stop sign. There are good views of Hawk Mountain on the right.
12.6	L	Make a left turn at the T onto Rabbit Run Road. At the time of this writing, there was no stop sign at this intersection. However, a hole where the sign might have been indicates we need to stop.
12.8	L	Make a left turn onto Reddale Road (unmarked).
16.75	BL	Bear left. Reddale Road becomes Lawrence Street.
17.0	R	Make a right turn onto Mifflin Street.
17.4	L	Make a left turn onto Warren Street.
17.5	END	End the ride at Warren and Market Streets.

FYI

Serenity Farm and Milk House, Orwigsburg (717-943-2919)

Bicycle Shops

Spokes Bike Shop, Route 61, Hamburg, PA (610-562-8900)

Weller's Bicycles, 1590 West Market Street, Pottsville, PA (717-622-2743)

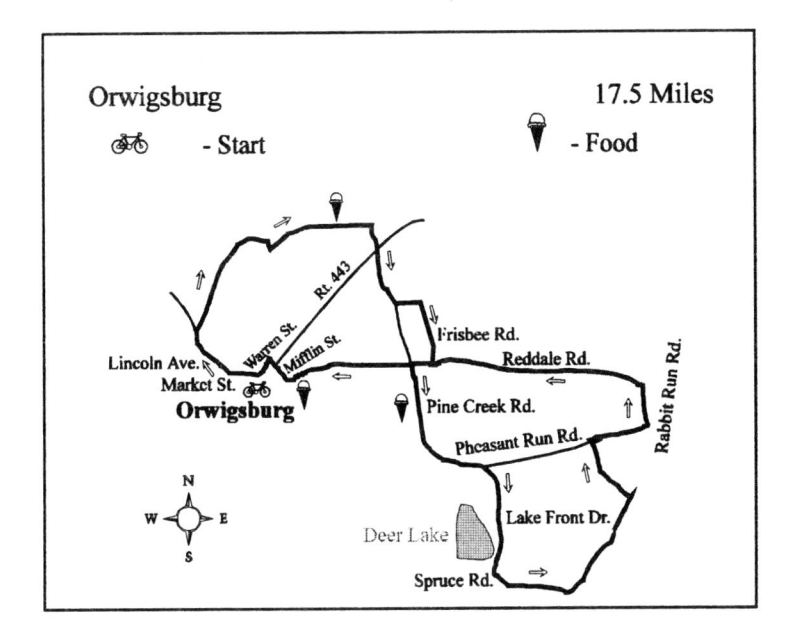

Orwigsburg

17.5 Miles

🚲 - Start 🍦 - Food